WHEN A
BABY DIES

SOME OTHER BOOKS BY RONALD NASH

The Concept of God

Faith and Reason: Searching for a Rational Faith

Worldviews in Conflict

Is Jesus the Only Savior?

*Why the Left Is Not Right: The Religious Left—Who
 They Are and What They Believe*

The Summit Ministry Guide to Choosing a College

The Gospel and the Greeks

Poverty and Wealth: Why Socialism Doesn't Work

*The Closing of the American Heart: What's Really
 Wrong with America's Schools*

The Word of God and the Mind of Man

Freedom, Justice and the State

*The Light of the Mind: St. Augustine's Theory of
 Knowledge*

The Meaning of History

RONALD H. NASH

WHEN A
BABY DIES

ANSWERS *to comfort*

grieving PARENTS

ZondervanPublishingHouse
Grand Rapids, Michigan

A Division of HarperCollins*Publishers*

When a Baby Dies
Copyright © 1999 by Ronald H. Nash

Requests for information should be addressed to:

 ZondervanPublishingHouse
Grand Rapids, Michigan 49530

Library of Congress Cataloging-in-Publication Data

Nash, Ronald H.
    When a baby dies : answers to comfort grieving parents / Ronald H.
  Nash.
       p. cm.
    Includes bibliographical references.
    ISBN 0-310-22556-6 (pbk.)
    1. Infant salvation. 2. Calvinism. I. Title.
  BT758.N37 1999
  234—dc21   98-39673
                                                              CIP

Interior design by Sherri L. Hoffman

Printed in the United States of America

99 00 01 02 03 04 05 06 /❖ DC/ 10 9 8 7 6 5 4 3 2 1

To Tamera and Jamie Cupschalk,
who encouraged me to write this book

CONTENTS

Prologue: When a Baby Dies   9

1. Are Children Born Without Sin?   13

2. Universalism: Will Everyone Be Saved?   23

3. Salvation After Death?   33

4. Does Baptism Save?   45

5. A Case for Infant Salvation   59

6. Infant Salvation: Some Theological Issues   71

7. The Reformed View of Infant Salvation   87

8. Some Final Questions   101

Epilogue: Heaven Scent   117

Notes   121

WHEN A BABY DIES

In the spring of 1997, James Cupschalk, a student in the seminary where I teach, shared a moving testimony of what he and his wife, Tamera, experienced in the birth and the death of their first child. Jim's words remind us that any investigation of the salvation of children who die in infancy must never lapse into abstraction and theory divorced from the importance of the young lives that have ended or from the personal pain and loss of their loved ones. What follows is James Cupschalk's story in his own words.[1]

"October 23, 1990, my wife and I entered the hospital delivery room. We waited in hope and anticipation of the life with which God would bless us, trying to be patient for the labor process to take its natural course. Finally, the next morning, the moment came and I watched proudly as my wife gave birth to our first child. It was a little girl. Yet, as soon as the excitement came, the tension of the room began to rise. She didn't seem to be breathing. Surely this was just a normal part of birth after being in the womb for the past nine months.

"The room became heavy as if a dense, hot haze had moved in. I watched the doctor pick up our baby's arm, expecting some reaction, but it fell to the table lifeless. The room was quiet except for the efforts of the doctors and nurses attempting to save the life of our little girl. I followed the orders of the nurse to follow her to the level two nursery, where I began to see that my daughter was not the perfect, healthy baby that we had hoped for.

"In the hall, the doctor grabbed me and said that he had seen circumstances like this before, and that there was not much hope for our baby. I acknowledged his comments but still clung to the hope that our baby would be an exception. In my wife's room, the geneticist came in and gave us his preliminary analysis. He, too, told us that the situation was hopeless.

"The time came for me to see my little girl. I went with my mother because my wife was still too weak to leave her room. I was very apprehensive, fearful about my reaction to seeing the deformed little body of my daughter. She had been moved to the neonatal intensive care unit, where I saw her for the first time since she had been born. When I saw her, I felt no fear, only peace and love for my little girl. This was my daughter and I loved her. As I went back to my wife's room, I had a new sense of hope and peace. I had seen and touched my little girl.

"On October 30, 1990, my wife and I received an early morning phone call. The hospital called to urge us to come quickly. Our daughter was not doing well, and they felt we should be with her. We arrived at the hospital, and the doctor explained that our baby had been through a very difficult night, and regardless of their attempts, her heart was failing and she was not getting enough oxygen. A nurse gave her to my wife, and she held our daughter, gently comforting her.

"We both knew that this was probably the last time we would see our daughter alive. The monitor showed only a straight line, and they disconnected the respirator. Her chest stopped moving, and my wife looked up to the nurse and asked if her heart was beating. Unable to get the words out, the nurse shook her head no. We moved to a small room reserved for families during times like these. I remember asking the nurse if I could remove the oxygen tube from her nose. It felt so good to hold her without all of the tubes and wires between us. I held her close to my heart, hugging, cuddling, and kissing her, feeling her little head against my cheek, brushing my lips against her soft hair.

"As my wife and I sat in that little room, we were convinced that God was in control of the situation and of our lives. Our little girl had struggled for six days, and on the seventh she rested."

WHAT LIES AHEAD?

It is difficult to read this testimony without feeling great empathy for the Cupschalks and any other parent who has lost a child. This book is an attempt to provide such parents and others in their immediate circle with answers to their most important questions.

I find that it is often helpful to provide my readers with a map of what lies ahead. If one is wandering through a jungle or a mountain pass, it is important to know where we're going and why.

The first four chapters explore several wrong approaches to the question of infant salvation. It is necessary to eliminate such beliefs before I lay out the case for my own position. These chapters will also help set certain boundaries within which an adequate set of answers must be located.

Chapter 1 explores the belief that infants are saved because they are born innocent of all sin.

Chapter 2 considers a couple of views that have been popular in theologically liberal segments of Christendom during much of the twentieth-century. The theories are variations of what is usually called *universalism*, the belief that all humans will eventually be saved.

Chapter 3 examines the teaching that when children die before they are able mentally and morally to be held responsible for their actions, the issue of their salvation is postponed until after they die.

Chapter 4 discusses critically the widely held belief that baptism saves from sin. It is regrettable how many within Christendom believe and teach that infants and the mentally incapable are saved from divine judgment by virtue of the fact that they have been baptized.

On the basis of these four chapters I argue that any theory about infant salvation must be rejected that ignores the fact of original sin, that claims that all human beings will someday be saved (universalism), that postpones the salvation of any human being to some imagined state after death, or that bases the salvation of any human being on an event such as baptism.

In chapter 5 I present and defend my own answer to the question of infant salvation.

Because theology is so important, chapters 6 and 7 will explore how this book's answer to the question of infant salvation fits into the often heated controversy between those evangelicals who emphasize human free will and humankind's ability to attain salvation (the position known as Arminianism) and the Reformed position that emphasizes God's sovereignty in salvation (Calvinism). Which theological system best provides consistent grounds for the salvation of infants and the mentally incapable that are faithful to Scripture?

Chapter 8, the last chapter of the book, offers answers to a number of related issues, such as what stage of moral and mental development ends the protective stage of infancy.

chapter one

ARE CHILDREN BORN WITHOUT SIN?

It is easy to understand why parents who lose a child seek some reason to ground the hope that their infant is saved. Unfortunately, many people seek this reason in false beliefs that not only lack any foundation in Scripture but that in fact contradict essential biblical claims. This is the first of four chapters to explore these false beliefs.

In three of these chapters I introduce the false theory in terms of a particular family's search for spiritual guidance and hope after the loss of a child. In each case, they mistakenly seek that help from a theological system that is inconsistent with Scripture. I do not do this to judge the parents. Many people justify their lack of biblical and theological knowledge by saying they have been too busy to pay attention to such matters. Denominational and theological differences have never seemed important to them, until suddenly, as in these cases, the tragic loss of a child makes it necessary to call on a minister for the funeral. In the stories that follow, all names are fictitious and, as they say in the movies, any resemblance between these people and any other person, living or dead, is purely coincidental.

In this chapter I critique a theory that continues to influence large numbers of people in Christendom, even though it was correctly denounced as a heresy almost sixteen hundred years ago. This belief, known as Pelagianism, teaches that all human beings are born morally innocent; infants are born without sin. Large numbers of people still seek mistakenly to ground the salvation of children who die in infancy upon their supposed sinlessness. This chapter explains why such thinking cannot be an option for Christians who regard the Bible as their ultimate authority of faith and practice. Whatever our answer to the issue of infant salvation, it must recognize that all human beings, including all infants, suffer from original sin.

SAM AND MARY

Sam and Mary are in their late twenties. They are a good example of what is often called an unchurched family. They met in college and were married in the church that Mary's family attended three or four times a year. The church building was large and ornate, although the small number of people in the typical Sunday morning service left much unfilled space in every row.

Even though Sam and Mary seldom attended church, they would always, when asked, say that they "belonged" to the big church in the center of town. Their first child was a beautiful little girl named Amy. One night when she was three, Amy came down with a fever that grew progressively worse as the night wore on. About three in the morning, Amy's condition became so critical that Sam and Mary rushed her to an emergency room. By 8 A.M., Amy was dead.

As though the shock of Amy's death were not bad enough, family members softly reminded them of the need to make funeral arrangements. Mary's mother called her pastor, Rev.

Michael Matthews, to request that he conduct Amy's funeral and also meet with Sam and Mary. The meeting was scheduled for the day before the funeral.

Reverend Matthews had studied at a small seminary in the East that was well-known for its liberal theology. By the time he graduated, he was grappling with a number of issues he had been unable to resolve during his seminary training. For one thing, he had lost his former confidence that the Bible was the Word of God. In place of the Bible, the real "Word of God" was the collection of subjective feelings, sentiments, and emotions that people sometimes become conscious of after reading the Bible. Sometimes similar feelings result from reading other literature, hearing certain forms of music, or observing works of art. Mike Matthews wasn't sure he understood how all this was supposed to work itself out in his preaching, but he was rather glad he didn't have to make his own beliefs and preaching adhere to everything in the Bible.

Because Mike had no ultimate, objective, and infallible religious authority, he wasn't sure what to believe about many issues, one of them being the matter of life after death. About the same year in seminary that he rejected the authority of the Bible, he had decided that the biblical account of the resurrection of Jesus Christ was historically untrue. He assumed that someone named Jesus had lived and died in Palestine. But he doubted that this Jesus was the eternal Son of God, the Second Person of the Trinity. He rejected the miracles attributed to Jesus in the New Testament and felt free to ignore any teachings of Jesus that no longer fit the worldview he had picked up during seminary. And Mike was quite agnostic on the matter of life after death.

Funerals always gave Mike problems. He knew he was supposed to eulogize the deceased and offer family members some hope for their loved one. He always found a way to be very ambiguous in his statements. He followed tradition and read the customary passages of Scripture such as Psalm 23 and Jesus' words, "In my Father's house are many mansions."

Amy's death confronted Mike with his first funeral for a child. He knew he could do and say most of the things that had become the major content of his funerals for adults. But what was he going to tell Sam and Mary at the conference they had requested?

When Sam and Mary sat down in Mike's study, their previous disinterest in Scripture and theology left them particularly vulnerable. They didn't even know the right way to phrase their question. They also had no knowledge of Reverend Matthews's theological doubts. Finally, their search for the right words produced the question that was on their hearts. "Reverend Matthews," they asked, "is Amy in heaven?"

If Mike had been totally honest at that moment, his answer would have been, "I don't know!" To be truthful, he didn't know whether there is a heaven or what it is like. But that did not seem an appropriate time or place to put his uncertainties into words. And so, without being consciously insincere, Mike smiled compassionately and said, "I am sure she is. If anyone is in heaven, I guarantee that Amy is."

Reverend Matthews leaned back in his chair, expecting that the meeting would soon end, now that he had answered the parents' question. But Sam and Mary were not finished. They wanted to know what heaven was like. Mike waved his hand, said something about how complex that question is, and expressed the hope that they might be able to meet again and discuss things like this on some other occasion. This time Mike was aware of his insincerity.

But once again, Sam and Mary were not through. They wanted some reason that would help ground their hope that Amy was in heaven. They even asked Mike for some verses from the Bible to support this belief. For the first time in their adult lives, Sam and Mary wanted an answer to a theological question. Mike was not used to people asking for biblical support for his religious claims. He hemmed and hawed for a minute or so while gathering his thoughts and then remembered something he had heard several of his seminary professors say. Ignoring Sam and Mary's request for biblical support, Mike tried to look confident as he said, "I'll tell you how we know Amy is in heaven. We know that all children are born innocent, without sin. Since Amy died in a totally sinless state, she and all children like her are fit subjects for heaven."

Unaware of how problematic Mike's words were, Sam and Mary thanked him and left. Mike relaxed, lit a cigar, leaned back in his chair, and congratulated himself on the brilliant way he maneuvered through that minefield. At 8 o'clock that evening, however, his phone rang. It was Mary. "Reverend Matthews, since Amy is in heaven, Sam and I want to be sure that we go to heaven when we die. But you said that Amy is in heaven because she died in a state of perfect moral innocence; she died without sin. But, Reverend Matthews, that won't work for Sam and me since both of us know that we've sinned. What must we do to get to heaven?" Mike excused himself by saying he was expecting another phone call and that he would get back to them in a day or two. After shutting off his portable phone, Mike reflected for a moment or two about the fact that he had never before used the word *sin* in his ministry. Well, he hadn't actually used it that day, either.

THE IMPORTANCE OF BEING INFORMED

Please remember that I am not being judgmental toward Sam and Mary. There are millions of Americans just like them, nice people and good parents who have been too busy to care about theology and the Bible. One of the first consequences of biblical and theological illiteracy is the inability to recognize the difference between ministers and churches that affirm and teach the historic Christian faith and those that deny it. All of us have heard the expression, "What you don't know *can* hurt you." It's surprising that more people haven't made the connection to ignorance about the Bible and theology.

If Sam and Mary had paid more attention to the Bible, they would have known that no one is born morally innocent, without sin.[1] If they had included the history of Christianity in their college studies, they would have known that Mike's answer has been around for at least fifteen hundred years. It is usually called *Pelagianism*, since the first major teacher of the doctrine, a British monk named Pelagius (died A.D. 418), carried the theory to Rome and North Africa in the early years of the fifth century.

As we will see in greater detail later in this book, the Bible teaches that every human being is born with a sinful nature. The theological term for this condition is *original sin*. It is the fact of original sin that explains why no human being needs to be taught how to sin. Sinning comes naturally to all of us because it is part of our nature. Every human, including every infant, suffers from original sin.

The fundamental idea behind Pelagianism is a denial of original sin. That is, no human being is born with a corrupted nature, with a natural bent toward sin. Children have no sinful tendencies that might lead them away from God. Humans are born morally neutral, neither sinner nor saint. Pelagius taught that Adam's sin affected only Adam himself. Hence, human infants are born innocent without any predisposition to sin. The view also implies that humans have the ability to please God, to satisfy God's criteria for salvation, without any assistance from God.

If infants and the mentally impaired were sinless, as Pelagianism teaches, there would be nothing in their nature to provoke God's judgment. The innocence of such infants is all that's needed to be an object of God's salvation. Every child can be saved for the simple reason that there is nothing in the child to merit condemnation.

Pelagius also taught that when children become mature enough to be moral agents, the choices of their later years lead in the direction of either good or evil. Whether the person chooses a righteous or sinful life is up to that person. Every human adult is a self-made creature.

I am not suggesting that ministers like Reverend Matthews are self-consciously Pelagian. Rather than their drawing their belief about inherent human innocence from Pelagius, it probably flows naturally from other liberal presuppositions picked up during their seminary days. After all, theological liberals like Reverend Matthews have been taught to dislike the word *sin*. For one thing, they consider the word judgmental. Moreover, in a world in which there may be no moral absolutes, it is hard to see how there can be any sin. While errors of judgment are possible, there can be no sin. It is easy, then, to understand the liberal's aversion to the notion of original sin.

But I have already made clear my intention to answer the question of infant salvation in a way that is consistent with the plain teaching of Scripture and a sound theology based on the Word of God.[2] Therefore I will now cite my objections to Pelagianism and base them on Scripture.

OBJECTIONS TO PELAGIANISM

Even though Pelagianism was denounced as a heresy by every church council following Pelagius's death, elements of his system have been incorporated into the teaching of many branches of Christendom. The objections that follow represent just a few of the reasons why the orthodox creeds of the Christian church have repudiated Pelagianism.

1. The claim of human sinlessness is clearly and forcefully denied through the Bible. Consider the following sampling of verses:

1 Kings 8:46: "There is no one who does not sin."

Psalm 143:2: "No one living is righteous before you [God]."

Proverbs 20:9: "Who can say, 'I have kept my heart pure; I am clean and without sin'?"

Ecclesiastes 7:20: "There is not a righteous man on earth who does what is right and never sins."

Romans 3:10, 12: "There is no one righteous, not even one. . . . there is no one who does good, not even one."

Romans 3:23: "For all have sinned and fall short of the glory of God."

1 John 1:8: "If we claim to be without sin, we deceive ourselves and the truth is not in us."

2. The Bible's repeated claim that all humans need forgiveness and salvation presupposes universal human sinfulness. "Salvation is found in no one else, for there is no other name under heaven given to men by which we must be saved" (Acts 4:12). God now "commands all people everywhere to repent" (Acts 17:30). Any student of Scripture will have no difficulty locating many other passages bearing the same message.

3. Scripture traces this universal human sinfulness back to the beginning of our existence. David wrote, "Surely I was sinful at birth, sinful from the time my mother conceived me" (Psalm 51:5). Psalm 58:3 tells us, "Even from birth the wicked go astray; from the womb they are wayward and speak lies."

Jesus taught that wicked actions are the manifestations of a sinful heart:

"Do people pick grapes from thornbushes, or figs from thistles? Likewise every good tree bears good fruit, but a bad tree bears bad fruit. A good tree cannot bear bad fruit, and a bad tree cannot bear good fruit" (Matthew 7:16–18).

Again, in Matthew 15:17–20, Jesus said,

"Don't you see that whatever enters the mouth goes into the stomach and then out of the body? But the things that come out of the mouth come from the heart, and these make a man 'unclean.' For out of the heart come evil thoughts, murder, adultery, sexual immorality, theft, false testimony, slander. These are what make a man 'unclean.'"

The Bible clearly opposes Pelagius's central idea that humans are born without sinful tendencies.

4. Even the most casual observance of the behavior of children shows that they never have to be taught to sin. Sinning comes as easily to children and adults as swimming to tadpoles or flying to birds. It is inherent in our nature.

5. Why do supposedly sinless, morally innocent infants who are supposedly born without sinful natures and tendencies always grow into sinful adults? Pelagians are obliged by the logic of their position to believe that at least a few sinless adults exist. The American news media might call Mother Teresa a saint, but she knew and confessed that she was a sinner. The biblical indictments of humankind noted above are supported by what each of us discovers when we honestly examine our own hearts: the phenomenon of human guilt.

CONCLUSION

This brief examination of the false belief that humans are born innocent, without sin and without corrupting influences, should make three points clear. First, if we are seeking an answer to the question of infant salvation that is based on Scripture, we cannot base our hope for infant salvation on the theory that infants are morally neutral and without sin. Second, to quote R. A. Webb, it is wrong to propose "a scheme of salvation in which neither Christ as an atoning sacrifice, nor the Spirit as a sanctifier, could have anything to do in saving children; for if children are salvable upon the ground of what they are not [that is, not sinners], they are not salvable upon the ground of what Christ has done for them, or the Spirit may do in them."[3] Third, wherever our search for an answer leads us, it must be consistent with the teaching of Scripture that all humans except Jesus Christ are born with a sinful nature.

It is clear, then, that any attempt to ground the salvation of infants and the mentally incapable on their supposed sinlessness is based on serious error and therefore we must turn elsewhere for an answer to our question.

chapter two

UNIVERSALISM: WILL
EVERYONE BE SAVED?

In this chapter I look at two other answers to the question of infant salvation often provided by religious liberals in American Protestantism. Once again, it will be convenient to follow the story of the Reverend Michael Matthews as a prototype of such liberals.

ROBERT AND BETTY

Robert and his wife, Betty, had a son, Robert Jr., with Down syndrome. They and their other children gave "young Bob" all the love and nurture it was possible for any family to provide. Robert, Betty, and their family attended Reverend Matthews's church faithfully. There were times when they were puzzled over why Reverend Matthews's sermons seemed so different from what they remembered about the small-town church they had grown up in. But they were busy with other things and had little time to study the sorts of things that would have helped them understand how Reverend Matthews's liberalism made it easy for him to spend little time explaining the Bible.

Mike's wife, Susan, had come from a solid Christian home, even though her beliefs had drifted far from those of her parents during college and Mike's years in seminary. Occasionally Susan would recall times during her childhood when her parents prayed and read the Scriptures aloud during family devotions. She had never shared these memories with Mike.

Even though Robert and Betty knew that young Bob might not live until his twentieth birthday, the boy's death at the age of sixteen came as a shock. Children with Down's tend to be loving and trusting kids and often become a source of great joy to their parents and siblings.

Naturally, Robert and Betty called on Reverend Matthews to lead the funeral service. They also asked if they might meet with him in his office the day after the funeral. Mike knew what they would ask during that visit. Mike had developed a close relationship with young Bob. When the phone call came confirming the boy's death, Mike wept. Mike admitted to Susan that at times like this he felt that his ministry was ineffective. He felt as if he really had nothing to say to people grieving over the loss of a loved one.

It wasn't long after the funeral of Sam and Mary's daughter that Mike began to seek a different answer to the question they had asked him about Amy's salvation. His new answer was part of an even more liberal shift in his theology. His earlier ambivalence about the Bible was now compounded by the conviction that God was simply unknowable. If anyone had ever asked Mike to identify three strong convictions, Mike would have answered that he was certain that Jesus Christ was only a human being, his death was not in any way a sacrifice for human sin, and if Jesus was a savior, it was only in a sense so general that the religion of his followers had no advantage over the salvation promised by other great religions.[1]

Susan knew that young Bob's death had caused Mike considerable pain. She found herself wondering what Mike might say at the funeral.

The next day, at the funeral, Mike surprised Susan by stating—quite dogmatically, she thought—that there was no question but that young Bob is in heaven. Mike then added, "And if you want a verse from the Bible to prove what I've just said, you'll find it in 1 John 4:8: 'God is love.' Those three words give the answer to most of life's difficult questions. Because it is obvious that a loving God would never allow one of his creatures to miss heaven, never permit one of his beloved creatures to suffer the torments of eternal punishment. Hence, we can know with absolute certainty that sooner or later, every member of our race will be saved. Young Bob is with the Lord at this moment because a loving God would not and could not allow any other situation to exist. Since a loving God will eventually bring all of his creatures, good or bad, to his heavenly home, we can know with absolute certainty that young Bob is in heaven."

Robert and Betty were not careful students of the Bible. As they turned to leave the committal service at the cemetery, each of them embraced Reverend Matthews and thanked him for his words of comfort. But Susan felt very uncomfortable and said nothing on the drive home. While she talked about various things during dinner and the early evening, she avoided bringing up her questions until after the evening news on television.

"Mike," she said, "I know this has been a terrible ordeal for you. But I won't find sleep very easy tonight unless you answer a few questions for me." Mike softly mumbled something that she took to mean "go ahead."

"Has your view of God changed since yesterday?"

"I don't believe so," Mike replied. "Why do you ask?"

"Do you still believe God is unknowable?"

"Sure, why not? What would lead you to ask such questions?"

Susan answered, "Today's sermon."

Without waiting for Mike to ask what she meant, Susan blurted out several questions without stopping: "If you still believe that God is unknowable, how can you say that God is love? If someone thinks God is unknowable, I should think it inconsistent to say anything meaningful about this unknowable God, such that it is love or that it is able to guarantee that even one person will exist forever, let alone the entire human race."

Mike just sat in his chair, saying nothing, so Susan kept going. "Weren't your words at the funeral today an endorsement of universalism?"

Mike nodded yes.

"How can you quote the Bible on one subject like the love of God and ignore what it says about universalism?"

Mike sighed. Internally he attributed his inability to think of a good response at that moment to his weariness and the lateness of the hour. So he kept his reply short. "Susan, as I sat here listening to you with my eyes closed, I could swear I was listening to your mother interrogate me, the way she used to when we were at the seminary. I'm too tired to think about questions like this tonight. I'm going bed. Perhaps these things won't seem quite so important to you in the morning."

Susan became aware of emotions she had not felt for years. She sat quietly on the sofa for a few minutes after Mike left the room. Suddenly she rose resolutely from the couch, went into another room, came back with a book in her hand, and started reading. It had been a long time since she had last read the Bible.

DOES MIKE UNDERSTAND THE LOVE OF GOD?

Susan's restlessness was caused by her sudden realization that Mike's religious beliefs were a hodgepodge of inconsistent points that he seemed incapable of sorting out. Susan was beginning to recognize serious conceptual difficulties in Mike's system of beliefs. While she thought she had abandoned the beliefs of her parents years ago, she suddenly found herself remembering that the faith of her mom and dad gave their lives and marriage a quality that she and Mike hadn't known in years. Her folks, for example, knew how to give grieving friends real comfort at funerals. The beliefs her parents shared not only came from the Scriptures but fit together in a way that made more sense to her during those years than anything she had believed since college. Without fully understanding it, Susan was beginning to move in a new direction. When she became more conscious, weeks later, of what was happening to her, she realized that it wasn't a new direction after all.

Not every religious liberal follows Mike's radical break with the Bible. More typically, men and women who are led away from historic Christianity still use the Bible to some degree. The catch is that they tend to treat the Bible seriously only when it agrees with their opinions. To a degree, this is what Mike began to do when he quoted the passage "God is love." When the Bible agrees with their opinions, liberals may even be willing to refer to it as "The Word of God." On those more numerous occasions when the Bible cannot be made to fit their preconceived opinions, it is not the Word of God.

However nice Mike's talk about universalism and the unqualified love of God might seem, neither position can be affirmed on scriptural grounds. Based on biblical standards, almost all of the content of Reverend Matthews's funeral sermon was false. It is important that we understand why.

Religious liberals in Christendom have typically elevated the love of God to a place of preeminence in their system. This is understandable. Talk about love makes us feel good, while talk about commandments, sin, punishment, and judgment does not. Many people prefer a religion that doesn't remind them of the Ten Commandments and the punishment God measures out to those who break his Law.

Scripture teaches that God possesses many attributes, all of which exist in perfect harmony. God's nature can never be in conflict. The attribute that unites all of God's properties is his holiness. Divine holiness qualifies every other property of God so that we should think of God's knowledge as holy knowledge, of his power as holy power, of his justice as holy justice, *and of his love as holy love.* One error in Reverend Matthews's thinking about God's love lay in separating love from God's other essential properties.

I suspect that much of the problem in all this lies in the fact that very few people have a clear understanding of what true holiness is. We sometimes talk rather glibly about living persons who are said to be "holy."

There is no comparison between the holiness and unqualified purity of God and anything in God's creation, especially human beings. Think of a blinding bright light that drives out all darkness. Think of an all-consuming fire that destroys all dross. Think of absolute, unqualified, unchanging, uncompromising purity and you might have grasped a fraction of God's holiness.

God's love must never be described in a way that makes it appear indifferent to human sin and guilt. The kind of love many liberals attribute to God is really just sappy sentimentalism. God's holy love is not separable from his wrath against sin and his judgment of sin. When two things or two people are moral opposites, God's holiness means that he cannot love both. If something is good and pure, the holy God loves it. If something is evil, God's holiness means that he hates it.

A FINAL WORD ABOUT UNIVERSALISM

All of Reverend Matthews's talk about the love of God in his funeral sermon was only a prelude leading up to his affirmation of universalism, the belief that eventually every human being will be saved.

It is unlikely that readers who are familiar with Scripture and regard the Bible as their ultimate rule of faith and practice are going to be fooled by universalism. If the Bible consistently and clearly proclaims that large numbers of human beings will be justly condemned and eternally lost, then people committed to universalism ought to be honest enough to admit that they have become proponents of a different religion than Christianity. The question for me at this point in the book concerns how much biblical evidence against universalism needs to be presented. There is merit, I think, in limiting most of my actual quotations to the words of Jesus.

In Matthew 7:13–14, part of the Sermon on the Mount, Jesus said,

> "Enter through the narrow gate. For wide is the gate and broad is the road that leads to destruction, and many enter through it. But small is the gate and narrow the road that leads to life, and only a few find it."

Jesus' clear warning is that many people are lost.

Later in the same chapter, Jesus issued a serious warning to apparently religious people:

> "Not everyone who says to me, 'Lord, Lord,' will enter the kingdom of heaven, but only he who does the will of my Father who is in heaven. Many will say to me on that day, 'Lord, Lord, did we not prophesy in your name, and in your name drive out demons and perform many miracles?' Then I will tell them plainly, 'I never knew you. Away from me, you evildoers!'" (Matthew 7:21–23).

Jesus' warning that even religious people who believe they are serving Christ can be lost is rather hard to square with a universalism that teaches that the most evil men and women in history will be saved. Of course, almost all contemporary universalists avoid that problem by ignoring the Bible.

In Matthew 8:11–12, Jesus describes the condition of the lost at the end of the world:

> "I say to you that many will come from the east and the west, and will take their places at the feast with Abraham, Isaac and Jacob in the kingdom of heaven. But the subjects of the kingdom will be thrown outside, into the darkness, where there will be weeping and gnashing of teeth."

Another serious warning from Jesus appears in Matthew 10:28: "Do not be afraid of those who kill the body but cannot kill the soul. Rather, be afraid of the One who can destroy both soul and body in hell."

Matthew 13 contains several parables, including the famous teaching about the wheat and the tares. A farmer planted good seed in his soil, but one night an enemy came and planted weeds. Jesus' explanation of the meaning of that parable contradicts universalism:

> "The one who sowed the good seed is the Son of Man. The field is the world, and the good seed stands for the sons of the kingdom. The weeds are the sons of the evil one, and the enemy who sows them is the devil. The harvest is the end of the age, and the harvesters are angels. As the weeds are pulled up and burned in the fire, so it will be at the end of the age. The Son of Man will send out his angels, and they will weed out of his kingdom everything that causes sin and all who do evil. They will throw them into the fiery furnace, where there will be weeping and gnashing of teeth" (Matthew 13:37–42).

John 3:17–18 is also important in this regard:

"For God did not send his Son into the world to condemn the world, but to save the world through him. Whoever believes in him is not condemned, but whoever does not believe stands condemned already because he has not believed in the name of God's one and only Son."

The awesome message here is that final and eternal condemnation is not just a possibility awaiting some terrible thing we have yet to do in our lives. The fact is, Jesus taught, that humans who do not believe in him are already condemned. John 3:36 brings this vitally important chapter to a close by reporting that "whoever believes in the Son has eternal life, but whoever rejects the Son will not see life, for God's wrath remains on him." The gift of eternal life is granted only to those who enter into a saving relationship with Jesus Christ, the Son of God. Those who reject the Son will be lost.

A short list of other passages can be consulted, including Luke 16:23–28; 2 Thessalonians 1:9; Jude 6; and Revelation 14:10–11. And, of course, there is the well-known passage from Revelation 20.

"Then I saw a great white throne and him who was seated on it. . . . And I saw the dead, great and small, standing before the throne, and books were opened. . . . Then death and Hades were thrown into the lake of fire. The lake of fire is the second death. If anyone's name was not found written in the book of life, he was thrown into the lake of fire" (Revelation 20: 11–15).

Since Scripture teaches that large numbers of the human race will be irredeemably lost, there is no possibility of building a case for human salvation on the supposed savability of the entire human race. And since this is true, neither universalism nor the liberal misrepresentation of divine love can provide an adequate ground for the salvation of deceased infants and mental incapables.

chapter three

SALVATION AFTER DEATH?

With this chapter, we leave Reverend Matthews and his liberal colleagues and turn our attention instead to a situation that could easily be encountered in a Baptist church, which just happens to be my own denomination. Since I need a fictional name for the Baptist preacher who will appear prominently in this chapter, suppose we call him Rev. Chuck Smith. That sounds like a good Baptist name.

Reverend Smith attended a large, well-known Baptist seminary in the early 1980s. What a lot of laypeople didn't know back then was how much liberal thinking had crept into some Baptist seminaries. When Chuck graduated from high school, he had a burning passion for missions and evangelism. There was a good chance, he thought, that after seminary he would apply to his denomination's foreign mission board and spend the rest of his life doing evangelism and establishing churches in some Third World country. Of course, at that time Chuck had no way of knowing how his theology professors at the Baptist seminary he selected would alter his plans.

During his seminary years some of Chuck's theology professors taught that humans who did not have an opportunity to accept the gospel during their lifetime would be given another chance to believe after death. Chuck decided he liked this view. About the same time, for rather obvious reasons, he gave up his plans to go to the mission field. After graduation, he accepted a call to be the pastor of a Baptist church in Colorado.

In his first two years in the pastorate Chuck didn't find much time to reflect on his seminary courses in theology. All of this changed when he was suddenly called on to preside over the funeral of a three-week-old baby. Chuck realized that relatives of the baby might ask him about the destiny of children who die in infancy, so he spent some time digging through his seminary notes. Understandably, the responsibilities of leading a funeral for a young child would produce nervousness in someone approaching this situation for the first time. This was quite different from cramming for a theology course at seminary.

The phone call came the afternoon before the funeral. Sandy and Jack, the baby's parents, asked if Chuck could stop by the house for prayer and counsel. Chuck knew what one of the questions would be.

After Chuck arrived, they sat around the kitchen table sipping coffee. It was Sandy who asked about her baby's future. Chuck smiled confidently and launched into his explanation of the theory of salvation after death he had learned in seminary. Chuck told Sandy and Jack that it would be wrong to believe that people who died without ever hearing the gospel were lost. After all, he said, the Bible teaches that millions of people like this would have an opportunity to hear the gospel after death. If they then trusted Christ as their Savior, they would be saved.

Jack interrupted the preacher by saying that during all his years attending Baptist churches, he had never heard this doctrine taught. Where, he asked, does the Bible teach this theory?

Chuck sat up straight, knowing this was a great opportunity for him to demonstrate his theological expertise and vast knowledge of Scripture. He was also pleased that his excep-

tional grasp of this new doctrine was making it possible for him
to provide real help to these two grieving parents.

"I'll show you where the Bible says all this. Let me read
some verses from 1 Peter chapters 3 and 4." Chuck then read
1 Peter 3:18–19 and explained that the verses teach that after
Jesus died, he descended into the underworld, where he
preached the gospel to dead souls that were in prison. He then
read 1 Peter 4:6 and explained that the verse teaches that people
who have died have the gospel preached to them. "That settles
it, then," Chuck said. "The Bible makes it clear that lots of
people will hear the gospel and be saved after they have died."

Sandy and Jack exchanged a glance that Chuck failed to
notice. Had you or I been seated around their kitchen table, we
would have sensed their bewilderment at Jack's detour into this
strange teaching. "That's all very interesting, Chuck," Sandy
said, "but what has any of this to do with our baby?"

"Don't you see," Chuck replied, "that children who die in
infancy are just like pagans who have never heard the gospel?
God will give such infants the same opportunity that 1 Peter
teaches he will give pagans."

This time Jack jumped in, his voice conveying some of his
frustration at what their original question had evoked. "But how
can any of this help our dead baby? She was only three weeks
old. She cannot understand the gospel. She cannot exercise saving faith."

Chuck offered his answer: "Obviously, when infants die,
they cannot comprehend the gospel and they are incapable of
saving faith. What happens during their time of opportunity
after death is that God brings them to a state where they are
mature enough to understand and believe. This guarantees that
every dead infant and mental incapable has a full opportunity
to hear and understand the gospel and then to exercise free will
either to accept or reject God's offer of salvation."

Jack knew that Sandy was getting very exercised over Chuck's theology lesson. "Tell me, Chuck," Sandy asked, "do all of these children end up believing the gospel, or do some of them reject it?"

Chuck wasn't prepared for this question, so he simply blurted out the first thing that came to mind. "God will never interfere with the free will of any of his creatures. Whether those children choose to believe or not to believe is their choice. I would like to think, however, that most of these children will in fact believe."

"But you do not know that they will," Jack asserted. Chuck had to admit that he didn't.

Sandy could no longer hide her exasperation. When they decided to ask Chuck to stop by the house, she never expected that the conversation would take this direction. She looked directly into Chuck's eyes and said, "You are telling us that the Bible teaches that the soul of our baby is in some kind of never-never land where God is allowing her to grow up in some way."

Feeling beads of perspiration on his forehead, Chuck had to admit that the Bible does not exactly teach anything corresponding to the situation Sandy just described.

"But," Sandy insisted, "that is precisely what you implied. Now you also tell us that when our baby's soul matures enough to understand the gospel, she will make a decision that will determine her eternal destiny. You are also telling us that Jack and I will go through the rest of our lives not knowing whether our little girl is saved or unsaved. Where did you get this stuff from?"

"I learned it at seminary," Chuck murmured.

At the funeral the next day, Chuck did not say anything about his seminary professor's theory on salvation after death. He pulled out his usual funeral sermon based on Psalm 23 and John 14. For some reason he found it difficult to look Jack and Sandy in the eye.

AN EVALUATION OF SALVATION
AFTER DEATH

For the record, Chuck's seminary doesn't teach salvation after death any more. Several years after he graduated, the seminary came under the control of more theologically literate board members who appointed a theologically conservative president. Within a relatively short time, many of Chuck's liberal professors had retired or taken positions at other schools. As important as these changes were, they came too late to help Chuck, who continues to identify with the liberal opinions of the faculty who controlled the school when he was a student.

Before his visit with Sandy and Jack, Chuck believed it would be easy to relate his theory about salvation after death to the case of deceased infants and the mentally handicapped. All he would have to do, Chuck thought, was suggest that these infants and mental incapables will be allowed somehow to mature to a point where they can understand the nature of sin, the difference between right and wrong, and the substance of the gospel. It would be a simple matter to claim that they would then be given an opportunity either to accept or to reject the gospel.

Many people, I suppose, might draw some comfort from this position, even as they conveniently ignore its serious liabilities. Let me summarize a few of these weaknesses.

1. First of all, proponents of this theory really seem to be just throwing in the towel and saying that the problem of infant salvation has no solution in this life. The entire issue of whether some infant is with the Lord following death is postponed to some unseen state that supposedly occurs after death.

2. The theory Chuck was taught clearly implies the possibility that large numbers of children will reject the gospel during the interval after death. This would result in their being

lost.[1] Hence, when pastors who hold this view lead the funerals of deceased infants, they can offer the parents no hope—indeed, no definitive word of any kind. The issue of the child's salvation is postponed until after death, with the outcome unpredictable.

3. As the rest of this chapter will make clear, all this is proposed without any scriptural support.

4. The theory falsely assumes that infants cannot be saved as infants. I will argue against this belief in later chapters.

DOES THE BOOK OF 1 PETER REALLY TEACH SALVATION AFTER DEATH?

Even though advocates of salvation after death typically appeal to 1 Peter 3:18–22 and 4:6 for support, the verses convey quite a different message. Let us examine both passages. First Peter 3:18–22 reads as follows:

> For Christ died for sins once for all, the righteous for the unrighteous, to bring you to God. He was put to death in the body but made alive by the Spirit, through whom also he went and preached to the spirits in prison[2] who disobeyed long ago when God waited patiently in the days of Noah while the ark was being built. In it only a few people, eight in all, were saved through water, and this water symbolizes baptism that now saves you also—not the removal of dirt from the body but the pledge of a good conscience toward God. It saves you by the resurrection of Jesus Christ, who has gone into heaven and is at God's right hand—with angels, authorities and powers in submission to him.

By any reckoning, this is a very difficult passage to interpret, perhaps one of the most difficult in all of Scripture.

Attempting to ground some important theological point on unclear and controversial texts is not exactly the best way to demonstrate one's theological competence. Wise Christians do not base any important doctrine—especially a controversial teaching that might also contain heretical implications—on one single, highly debatable passage of Scripture. The principle of allowing clear passages to interpret ambiguous ones, of allowing doctrinal passages to interpret nondoctrinal ones, of allowing clearly literal passages to interpret material full of nonliteral language is well-established. But let us continue.

In the verses that follow this passage (1 Peter 4:1–5), Peter writes of how Christians reject the wicked lifestyle of the unsaved. Because of this rejection, Christians suffer abuse from the unsaved, who one day will stand before the Judge of the living and the dead. Then in verse 6, Peter writes: "This is the reason the gospel was preached even to those who are now dead, so that they might be judged according to men in regard to the body, but live according to God in regard to the spirit."

Teachers of the salvation-after-death theory try desperately to link 1 Peter 4:6 and its supposed comment about preaching to the dead with the references to Noah's ark and "the spirits in prison" in chapter 3. This tactic is greatly weakened by the way that 1 Peter 4:1–5 slips alien subject matter into the middle of what post-death salvationists want everyone to believe is one unbroken line of thought. We must ask why these five verses are allowed to interrupt what is supposed to be an unbroken discourse on a different subject. These five verses make it extremely unlikely that 1 Peter 4:6 and its reference to preaching to those now dead is somehow connected with 1 Peter 3:18–22.

When 1 Peter 4:6 says that "the gospel was preached even to those who are now dead," does it mean that there is salvation after death? There are three good reasons to think not.

1. The after-death salvationist reading of 1 Peter 4:6 is an implausible reading of the verse because of the contradiction it produces in Christian thought. Second Corinthians 5:10 is only one of many biblical passages that teach that God's final judgment is based on the things that we did in our body, that is, in this earthly life.[3] If the theory of salvation after death is allowed to stand without challenge, it would introduce a major contradiction into Scripture.

2. There is no reason to think that the "dead" mentioned in 1 Peter 4:6 are identical with "the spirits in prison" mentioned in 1 Peter 3. The long interval in 1 Peter 4:1–5 breaks any supposed continuity between the two passages.

3. There are at least two more plausible interpretations: (a) "Those who are now dead" in 4:6 more naturally refers to people who were spiritually dead at one time and became spiritually alive after hearing the gospel. This is precisely the analogy Paul presents in Ephesians 2:1–10; (b) alternatively, "those who are now dead" may well be people who heard the gospel during their lifetime but who are now, at the time of writing, deceased.

What about 1 Peter 3:19–22, quoted earlier, which states that through the Spirit, Christ also "went and made proclamation to the spirits now in prison, who once were disobedient, when the patience of God kept waiting in the days of Noah" (NASB)? What does this mean? This verse is often injected into the debate because post-death salvationists understand it to say that between Jesus' death and resurrection he descended into the lower world and evangelized some group of people who were already dead. The reason this view does not work is that verse 20 appears to describe the recipients of Christ's message as unbelievers who lived during the time of Noah. Did Jesus preach to these unbelievers back before the Flood? But why would he preach only to unbelievers in that situation? Why did he not also preach to the believing patriarchs of the Old Testament, who could have profited from what he had to say? And why did he preach only before the Flood? All these questions suggest that the interpretation under consideration is badly off track.

Some understand 1 Peter 3 to say that Christ preached to the lost while he was alive, and those lost people were figuratively in prison; and that Christ's preaching to the lost was analogous to Noah's preaching to the lost before the Flood. Another plausible interpretation suggests that 1 Peter 3:19 speaks of how the Spirit of Christ (1 Peter 1:11) spoke through Noah (2 Peter 2:5) to men and women who are now in a prison of judgment. They were judged for their disobedience and are suffering the consequences. Through Noah's preaching they were exposed to the light, but they rejected it. In neither of these more plausible interpretations is there the slightest indication of any chance at salvation after death.

There is another good reason why 1 Peter 3 *cannot* teach any kind of salvation after death. The context finds Peter urging Christians to remain faithful to the work of witnessing and evangelism in spite of persecution. It makes little sense for Peter to say this and at the same time tell the persecuted Christians that the unbelievers behind all their suffering will have a second chance to be saved after they die.

POST-DEATH JUDGMENT IS BASED ON PRE-DEATH CONDUCT

The New Testament offers no hope beyond the grave for people who die in a lost condition. On the contrary, it consistently teaches that physical death is the end of any opportunity for salvation. This can be seen, for example, in Matthew 7:13–14, in which Jesus warns his listeners of the broad road and the wide gate that lead to destruction, and then urges them to be among the few who enter the narrow gate and follow the narrow road that leads to life. There is no suggestion of an opportunity for salvation after death in these words.

In Matthew 7:15–20, Jesus warns of false prophets who would come in sheep's clothing. He concludes by saying, "Every tree that does not bear good fruit is cut down and thrown into the fire." The predicted judgment will be based on deeds done during one's earthly life.

In Matthew 7:21–23, Jesus speaks of those who will come to him at the judgment, saying, "Lord, Lord, did we not prophesy in your name, and in your name drive out demons and perform many miracles?" In response, Jesus says, he will tell them plainly, "I never knew you. Away from me, you evildoers!" Once again, postmortem judgment is based on premortem conditions. The same point appears in Matthew 7:24–27, Jesus' well-known story of the men who built their respective houses on rock and sand.

We would do well also to study Jesus' parables related in Matthew 13. Explaining the parable of the weeds (vv. 24–30, 36–43), Jesus says, "As the weeds are pulled up and burned in the fire, so it will be at the end of the age. The Son of Man will send out his angels, and they will weed out of his kingdom everything that causes sin and all who do evil." The sin and evil referred to pertain to things done prior to death. There are no qualifications in this or other passages; there are no hints of exceptions arising from events after death.

While we are examining Jesus' teaching, we should look at his story of the rich man and Lazarus in Luke 16:19–31. Advocates of salvation after death often attempt to dismiss this passage. After all, they say, it is a parable, and we all know how difficult parables can be to interpret. But note that the objection to using this parable comes from the same people who rest almost their entire case for postmortem salvation on a highly imaginative interpretation of 1 Peter 3–4. The post-death salvationist's major line of argument against those who think Luke 16:19–31 is relevant to the issue of judgment after death is to claim that the parable's context suggests the story's primary message deals with improper uses of wealth. But even if this were so, the parable's lessons about judgment after death are hardly incidental and irrelevant. After all, this story was told by the Master Teacher, who could hardly have been unaware of how easily the details would lead many to form judgments about the status of the rich man and Lazarus following their deaths. Luke 16:19–31 cannot easily be dismissed as a source for the belief that postmortem judgment is based on premortem conditions.

By way of conclusion, it is worth remembering Hebrews 9:27: "It is appointed for mortals to die once, and after that the judgment" (NRSV).[4] When the day of judgment comes, it will be terrible to behold. That day of judgment is described in Revelation 20:11–13:

> Then I saw a great white throne and him who was seated on it. Earth and sky fled from his presence, and there was no place for them. And I saw the dead, great and small, standing before the throne, and books were opened. Another book was opened, which is the book of life. The dead were judged according to what they had done as recorded in the books. The sea gave up the dead that were in it, and death and Hades gave up the dead that were in them, and each person was judged according to what he had done.

Surely the intent of Hebrews 9:27 and Revelation 20:11–13 is to show that the judgment of each human being reflects that person's standing with God at the moment of death. Postmortem judgment is based on premortem conditions.

CONCLUSION

In all these passages and more, one simple point stands out: Physical death marks the boundary of human opportunity for salvation. Anyone who wishes to argue that Jesus and the authors of the New Testament believed otherwise must shoulder the burden of proof. Given the serious implications of a belief in postmortem salvation, the total silence of Scripture regarding opportunities after death should trouble Christians who claim to base their beliefs upon Scripture.

It is true, of course, that the discussion of the past few pages focuses on biblical passages that deal primarily with the death and judgment of adults. But if there is no biblical warrant for believing that adults can be saved after death, the case for believing that infants have such an opportunity collapses. There is no biblical warrant for believing that any human, adult or child, will be judged on the basis of something that happens after death.[5]

chapter four

DOES BAPTISM SAVE?

No discussion of infant salvation can be complete if it ignores the doctrine of baptismal regeneration. According to this teaching, God uses the means of water baptism to produce the inward change in the human heart that theologians call *regeneration*. Children or adults who have not been baptized are not saved, they are not born again, and their sins are not forgiven. Water baptism is a necessary condition for the new birth.

THE DOCTRINE OF BAPTISMAL REGENERATION

A number of denominations teach some version of baptismal regeneration. While there are occasional differences between them, it would serve no good purpose in this book to get involved in a highly technical discussion of the subject. I have chosen to keep my treatment of this issue simple. My objectives in the chapter are (1) to show that many people attempt to "solve" the problem of infant salvation by basing it on a belief in baptismal regeneration; (2) to argue that the biblical passages usually cited in support of this belief do not teach this doctrine; and (3) to show therefore that we must look elsewhere for biblical and theological support for infant salvation.

A number of Protestant denominations either teach baptismal regeneration explicitly or approach the subject in such a way that large numbers of their communicants believe the doctrine. Lutheranism, the church in which I was raised and baptized as a child, has historically affirmed baptismal regeneration. The doctrine can be found in Martin Luther's Catechism: "It [Baptism] worketh forgiveness of sins, delivers from death and the devil, and gives everlasting salvation to all who believe, as the Word and the promise of God declare."[1] It is also taught in Lutheranism's *Augsburg Confession:* "Of Baptism, they [Lutherans] teach that it is necessary to salvation, and that by Baptism the grace of God is offered, and that children are to be baptized, who by Baptism, being offered to God are received into God's favour."[2] While British Anglicanism and American Episcopalianism contain diverse streams of theological thought, members of this branch of Christendom who follow high church sacramentarianism affirm baptismal regeneration. The belief is also shared by members of other denominations in America and Great Britain.

The Roman Catholic Church is the largest religious body teaching baptismal regeneration. Its doctrine affirms that removal of human sin depends on the sacrament of baptism. Without baptism, no child or adult can be saved. The Canons and Dogmatic Decrees of the Council of Trent (1563) based the salvation of infants on Roman Catholic baptism.[3] In 1951, Pope Pius XII taught that "no other way besides Baptism is seen of imparting the life of Christ to little children."[4] The *New Catholic Encyclopedia* states: "By Christian Baptism one enters into the kingdom of God and into the sphere of the saving work of Christ."[5] Roman Catholic thinkers typically cite John 3:5 as their primary biblical support for their belief.[6]

THE CASE AGAINST BAPTISMAL
REGENERATION

Presbyterian theologian R. A. Webb opposed the doctrine of baptismal regeneration almost a century ago. We should hardly find it surprising, he wrote, that so many people attempt to find salvation in ceremonies and rituals. Webb observed,

> The natural opposition of the human heart to the principles and schedules of the divine procedure in the salvation of sinners, the natural tendency to construe the scheme of redemption in such a manner as will reflect credit upon mankind, rather than in a mode humbling to human pride and religious conceit, has appeared in two historical forms: (a) in a tendency to rely upon what men are, have done, or can do; and (b) in a tendency to rely upon the intervention of other men in the administration of outward and sensible ordinances.

The first of Webb's options is "the tendency to get the blessings of religion for ourselves... [while] the other is the tendency to get these blessings through priestly intermediaries."[7]

The Pelagian position we encountered in chapter 1 is one example of Webb's first position. Webb's first option is also typified by religious systems that teach that humans can be saved by their effort and good deeds. Webb's second option is represented in churches such as Roman Catholicism and high church Episcopalianism that offer salvation through sacraments such as baptism. Both positions, Webb writes, drift "away from a simple and sound evangelicalism, which bottoms upon the proposition, that whatsoever is not commanded in the Scriptures, either explicitly or by good and necessary consequences, is forbidden to be prescribed as a dogma for faith on the one hand, or as a precept for worship and discipline on the other."[8]

If baptism is a necessary condition for the salvation of any infant, it ought to be obvious that the doctrine of infant salvation offers little or no hope for the millions of unbaptized infants who have died over the centuries.[9] It is not enough simply to note that baptismal regeneration leaves millions of unbaptized infants in great spiritual jeopardy. In the rest of this chapter I will argue that baptismal regeneration cannot offer any hope for baptized children, either, since the doctrine is *not* taught in Scripture.

THE CONSISTENCY OF BIBLICAL TEACHING

If some passage of Scripture can be interpreted in two different ways and one of those interpretations is in clear conflict with the rest of Scripture, the interpretation that produces the contradiction should be rejected. The doctrine of baptismal regeneration *is* contradicted by the plain teaching of Scripture. Once that fact is established, we can approach the so-called problem texts with the confidence that they cannot possibly teach baptismal regeneration.

1. According to Scripture, there is only one necessary condition for salvation, and that is faith in Jesus Christ. Note the following passages:

> "For God so loved the world that he gave his one and only Son, that whoever believes in him shall not perish but have eternal life. . . . Whoever believes in him [Jesus] is not condemned, but whoever does not believe stands condemned already because he has not believed in the name of God's one and only Son." . . . Whoever believes in the Son has eternal life, but whoever rejects the Son will not see life, for God's wrath remains on him (John 3:16, 18, 36).

Then Jesus declared, "I am the bread of life. He who comes to me will never go hungry, and he who believes in me will never be thirsty.... For my Father's will is that everyone who looks to the Son and believes in him shall have eternal life, and I will raise him up at the last day" (John 6:35, 40).

Jesus said to her, "I am the resurrection and the life. He who believes in me will live, even though he dies; and whoever lives and believes in me will never die" (John 11:25–26).

In answer to the Philippian jailer's question of what he must do to be saved, Paul and Silas replied, "Believe in the Lord Jesus, and you will be saved" (Acts 16:31).

Everyone who believes that Jesus is the Christ is born of God, and everyone who loves the father loves his child as well.... Who is it that overcomes the world? Only he who believes that Jesus is the Son of God (1 John 5:1, 5).

2. In 1 Corinthians 1:14, Paul tells the church at Corinth, "I am thankful that I did not baptize any of you except Crispus and Gaius." If Paul believed and taught that baptism was absolutely essential to the new birth, his failure to baptize more than two people in Corinth is an odd thing to boast about. The obvious inference is that baptism is not a precondition for salvation.

3. Romans 2:28–29 declares, "A man is not a Jew if he is only one outwardly, nor is circumcision merely outward and physical. No, a man is a Jew if he is one inwardly; and circumcision is circumcision of the heart, by the Spirit, not by the written code." According to this verse, external physical acts like circumcision *and baptism* do not effect regeneration. Regeneration is a matter of the heart and the Holy Spirit.

TWO TEXTS THAT LINK REGENERATION
AND WATER

The word *regeneration* is an important theological term that many people have trouble defining. In an important sense, the terms *new birth* and *regeneration* describe the same event by which God takes sinful men and women and turns them into children of God who now possess his nature. Note the important *before* and *after* as described by the apostle Paul: "For if [the before], when we were God's enemies, we were reconciled to him through the death of his Son, how much more, having been reconciled [the after], shall we be saved through his life!" (Romans 5:10). As Jesus made clear, this transformation cannot occur unless we are born again (John 3:3). Being regenerated by the power of God, we are transformed so that we are now partakers of God's own nature, a fact that explains why God can truly regard us as children of God (1 John 3:1).

As we know, advocates of baptismal regeneration teach that baptism is the only means by which we receive this regeneration or new birth. When advocates of this view are challenged to provide biblical support for the teaching, the verses they usually cite first are Titus 3:5 and the third chapter of John's gospel. Since John 3 is the more important passage, demonstrating that it does not teach baptismal regeneration will make it a simple matter to show the futility of any appeal to Titus 3:5.

The relevant verses in John 3 read as follows:

> Now there was a man of the Pharisees named Nicodemus, a member of the Jewish ruling council. He came to Jesus at night and said, "Rabbi, we know you are a teacher who has come from God. For no one could perform the miraculous signs you are doing if God were not with him."
>
> In reply Jesus declared, "I tell you the truth, no one can see the kingdom of God unless he is born again."

"How can a man be born when he is old?" Nicodemus asked. "Surely he cannot enter a second time into his mother's womb to be born!"

Jesus answered, "I tell you the truth, no one can enter the kingdom of God unless he is born of water and the Spirit" (John 3:1–5).

Proponents of baptism regeneration make a huge leap at this point. First, they assume that being "born of water" is identical with the baptism that Jesus would institute after his resurrection (Matthew 28:19). Second, they assume that baptism necessarily produces regeneration (being "born of the Spirit"). Both of these assumptions are wrong.

A little reflection on the historical context of the encounter with Nicodemus should reveal why the effort to turn Jesus' use of the word *water* into a reference to baptism is faulty. For one thing, note that the word *baptism* never appears once, either in John 3 or Titus 3:5. Let us call this fact Strike One. An analogous error might lead the Wonder Bread company to tout the virtues of its product via a television commercial showing a scene of an actor portraying Jesus as he uttered the words, "I am the bread of life."

Nicodemus at that time and place in history could not have understood "water" to mean baptism. Even if Nicodemus had heard of Jesus' baptism by John the Baptist (and this is highly unlikely), any inference from Jesus' words to the baptism of John would have produced a false conclusion. Even if (contrary to fact), John 3 did contain a clear reference to baptism, it could not have been the baptism of John. The New Testament is clear that Christian baptism and the baptism of John are totally different acts. John's baptism was a baptism unto repentance. The disciples consciously refused to recognize John's baptism as equivalent to Christian baptism; they insisted that followers of

John be rebaptized (Acts 19:1–6). Jesus could not have meant the phrase "born of water" as a reference to John's form of baptism. Let us call this Strike Two.

Nicodemus could not have understood Jesus' words as a reference to Christian baptism. Initiation of the practice was still several years in the future. Jesus himself baptized no one, and his disciples did not baptize before Pentecost. Never once prior to his crucifixion did Jesus mention the water baptism that the disciples would institute at Pentecost. If baptism really were necessary for salvation, consider how strange it is that Jesus ignores the practice in his final words to his disciples (John 14–17). Let us call this Strike Three.

Since Nicodemus would not have interpreted Jesus' mention of "water" as baptism, what would Jesus' references to "water and the Spirit" have meant to someone like Nicodemus? What should the terms mean to us today?

Charles Hodge, a nineteenth-century professor of theology at Princeton Theological Seminary, argued that John 3:5 sets up an analogy between the way water cleanses the body and the way the Holy Spirit cleanses the soul. "[T]o be born of water and of the Spirit, is to experience a cleansing of the soul analogous to that effected for the body by water."[10] In the pages of Scripture, Hodge continues, "the sign and the thing signified are often united, often interchanged, the one being used for the other."[11] For examples, see Isaiah 35:6; 55:1; Jeremiah 2:13; and John 4:10; 7:37–38.

So here we have a clash between two interpretations: (a) being "born of water" is a reference to the saving efficacy of baptism; and (b) the allusion to water is a comparison of the cleansing effect water has on the body and the cleansing power of the Holy Spirit on the human heart. The effort to read baptismal regeneration into John 3 not only contradicts the dominant biblical emphasis on faith as the instrument of salvation, but also forces us to ignore the historical context. The competing inter-pretation offered by thinkers like Hodge is consistent with the rest of Scripture and fits the context much more naturally.

The same principle applies in the case of Titus 3:4–7, which reads as follows:

> But when the kindness and love of God our Savior appeared, he saved us, not because of righteous things we had done, but because of his mercy. He saved us through the washing of rebirth and renewal by the Holy Spirit, whom he poured out on us generously through Jesus Christ our Savior, so that, having been justified by his grace, we might become heirs having the hope of eternal life.

Paul never waters down (pun intended) the gospel of grace. Humans are never saved by *anything* that they have done. Our salvation is based totally and exclusively on God's unmerited favor—that is, grace. This rebirth, renewal, or regeneration comes about through the work of the Holy Spirit. The word "washing" in verse 5 does not refer to water touching the body but refers instead to the inner cleansing brought about by the Holy Spirit.

It is clear then that being "born of water" is an analogy that tells us that just as water cleanses the body, so the Holy Spirit cleanses the soul. Neither John 3 nor Titus 3 includes any reference to baptism, let alone to baptismal regeneration.

WHAT ABOUT ACTS 22:16 AND 2:38?

The futile quest for a biblical basis for baptismal regenera-tion eventually turns to a few other Scriptures. One of these is Acts 22:14–16, where Paul tells about his blinding encounter with Christ on the road to Damascus. After Paul, still sightless, was taken to Damascus, Ananias said to him, "The God of our

fathers has chosen you to know his will and to see the Righteous One and to hear words from his mouth. You will be his
witness to all men of what you have seen and heard. And now
what are you waiting for? Get up, be baptized and wash your
sins away, calling on his name."

Are we really supposed to believe that Paul's sins were not
forgiven until his moment of baptism? Charles Hodge chal-
lenges such an interpretation. This reading of Ananias's words,
Hodge writes,

> would contradict the plainest teachings of Scripture; as Paul
> himself says that God called him by his grace, and made
> him a true Christian by revealing his Son in him, by open-
> ing his eyes to see the glory of God in the face of Jesus
> Christ, which revelation attended the vision he had on his
> way to Damascus; and as the effect of that spiritual revela-
> tion was to transform his whole nature and lead him to fall
> to the ground, and say, "Lord, what wilt thou have me to
> do?" no one can believe that he was under the wrath and
> curse of God, during the three days which intervened
> between his conversion and his baptism. He did not receive
> baptism in order that his sins should be washed away; but as
> the sign and pledge of their forgiveness on the part of God.

Hodge concludes, "This passage is perfectly parallel to Acts
2:38, where it is said, 'Repent, and be baptized every one of you
in the name of Jesus Christ for the remission of sins.'. . . The
remission of sins was that to which baptism was related; that of
which it was the sign and seal."[12]

To sum up, neither Acts 22:16 nor 2:38 teaches baptismal
regeneration. In Acts 2:38, the Spirit had already descended
upon the people. They were regenerate believers. In interpret-
ing Acts 22:16, we must remember that Paul's conversion
occurred on the road to Damascus.

MARK 16:15 – 16

The verses read as follows: "He [Jesus] said to them, 'Go into all the world and preach the good news to all creation. Whoever believes and is baptized will be saved, but whoever does not believe will be condemned.'"

There are enormous problems in appealing to this verse as support for baptismal regeneration. One of those problems is explained in the New International Version of the Bible, where there is a line after Mark 16:8, followed by these words: "The most reliable early manuscripts and other ancient witnesses do not have Mark 16:9–20."[13]

The same disputed group of texts contains the verse (Mark 16: 18) that snake-handlers in Appalachia appeal to in support of their use of poisonous serpents in religious services.

Knowledgeable Christians recognize the risks involved in any attempt to base some important doctrinal claim on a verse that may not be part of the original manuscripts.

However, even if Mark 16:15–16 were not a debatable passage, the verses are no more help to the supporters of baptismal regeneration than anything else we have examined. There are a number of plausible reasons why baptism and salvation are linked in passages like this and the texts in Acts already noted. By the time these New Testament books were written, Christian baptism had been instituted. Not only that, it became the outward and observable symbol of the cleansing that takes place in an inward and nonobservable way. Once again, notice Mark 16:15–16: "Go into all the world and preach the good news to all creation. Whoever believes and is baptized will be saved, *but whoever does not believe will be condemned.*" The last clause is the relevant one here. It does not say, "Whoever is not baptized will be condemned." It reads, "Whoever does not believe will be condemned." The last clause makes clear that baptism and salvation are not irrevocably linked.

Christendom is full of baptized people. As Jesus teaches in the parable of the wheat and the tares (Matthew 13:24–30; 36–43), things are not always what they seem. It takes no great powers of observation to detect that water baptism, at whatever age it is administered, has never guaranteed salvation. There will be many baptized people in hell. Charles Hodge writes, "The doctrine of the Bible . . . is that he is not a Christian who is one outwardly, but that he is a Christian who is one inwardly; and the baptism which saves the soul is not baptism with water, but the baptism of the heart by the Holy Ghost."[14] The baptism of the Holy Spirit is the condition of regeneration (1 Corinthians 12:13); water baptism is the outward symbol of the inner cleansing (Romans 6:1–11).

Charles Hodge concludes,

> The two great errors against which the Gospel, as taught by Christ and unfolded by his apostles, was directed; were first the doctrine of human merit; the merit of good works, the doctrine that men are to be saved on the ground of their own character or conduct; and the second was ritualism, the doctrine of the necessity and inherent supernatural virtue of external rites and ceremonies. . . . the great burden of apostolic teaching was first, that we are saved, not by works but by faith, not for our own righteousness, but on the ground of the righteousness of Christ; and secondly, that religion is a matter of the heart, not of ritual or ceremonial observances.[15]

According to Hodge, the doctrine of baptismal regeneration "changes the whole nature of religion. It makes mere external observances the conditions of salvation, assuming that outward rites are exclusively the channels through which the benefits of redemption are conveyed to the souls of men. It excludes from the hope of heaven men who truly believe, repent and lead a holy life; and it assures those of their title to eternal life, who are unrenewed and unsanctified."[16] It is a serious distortion of biblical truth to make an outward ceremony such as baptism a necessary condition for regeneration.

CONCLUSION

The doctrine of baptismal regeneration is a serious error because it gives false hope to adults who think either they or their children are suited for heaven because of a ceremony that happened sometime in the past. The doctrine seriously distorts God's plan of redemption. It also entails that unbaptized infants who die are lost simply because they failed to receive one or more sacraments of the church. The mistaken and unbiblical belief in baptismal regeneration must not be thought to ground the salvation of children who die in infancy.

chapter five

A CASE FOR INFANT
SALVATION

The four chapters about false approaches to the issue of infant salvation have established the truth of four propositions:

1. No theory of infant salvation can be biblically sound if it ignores the way original sin leaves all humans including infants and the mentally incapable both guilty and depraved. All infants and mental incapables need salvation.

2. If deceased infants and the mentally incapable are saved, it must be on the basis of Christ's atonement.

3. If deceased infants and the mentally incapable are saved, it can only be because they have been regenerated and sanctified by the grace of God.

4. If deceased infants and the mentally incapable are saved, their salvation must occur before death.

THE AUTHOR'S POSITION

It is now time to identify the position that I will defend in the rest of this book. I will argue *that all children who die in infancy and all mentally handicapped persons whose intellectual and moral judgment cannot surpass that of children are saved.*[1] This chapter will build a case for my position on the basis of four well-established biblical claims. However, the significance of one of these claims may not become clear to every reader until we reach the end of chapter 7.

1. INFANTS ARE INCAPABLE OF MORAL GOOD OR EVIL

Scripture declares that infants do not know good or evil (Deuteronomy 1:39). Infants therefore lack the ability to perform morally good or morally evil acts. Scripture even describes infants as "innocent" (Jeremiah 19:4). It should be obvious that the use of the word *innocent* in this connection must be consistent with what we have already learned about the sinful nature of young children. Infants are innocent in the sense that whatever their natural disposition to sin may be, their status as infants makes it impossible for them to know or understand the things that would be necessary for them to perform good or evil acts. Therefore they are not moral agents. All these statements apply with equal force to the mentally impaired.

2. DIVINE JUDGMENT IS ADMINISTERED ON THE BASIS OF SINS COMMITTED IN THE BODY

God's condemnation is based on the actual commission of sins. This important point is taught throughout Scripture. Second Corinthians 5:10 states, "For we must all appear before the judgment seat of Christ, that each one may receive what is due him for the things done while in the body, whether good or bad." Note the clear statement that the final judgment is based on sins committed during our earthly existence. Note further that since infants are incapable of being moral agents, since they die before they are able to perform either good or evil acts,[2] deceased infants cannot be judged on the criterion specified in this verse.

In 1 Corinthians 6:9–10, Paul provides a list of people who will not enter heaven:

> Do you not know that the wicked will not inherit the kingdom of God? Do not be deceived: Neither the sexually immoral nor idolaters nor adulterers nor male prostitutes nor homosexual offenders nor thieves nor the greedy nor drunkards nor slanderers nor swindlers will inherit the kingdom of God.

There is no reason to regard this list as complete; one can easily think of a host of related sins, all of which violate at least one of God's Commandments. It is easy to see that infants and mental incapables cannot perform such deeds.

Revelation 20:11–12 makes the same point even as it adds more detail:

> Then I saw a great white throne and him who was seated on it. Earth and sky fled from his presence, and there was no place for them. And I saw the dead, great and small, standing before the throne, and books were opened. Another book was opened, which is the book of life.

There is no support for the claim of some that the words "great and small" refer to adults and children. The reference is to the powerful and weak, the famous and unknown, those puffed up with their own self-importance and common people often regarded as insignificant.

The passage in Revelation 20 then reports, "The dead were judged according to what they had done as recorded in the books. The sea gave up the dead that were in it, and death and Hades gave up the dead that were in them, and each person was judged according to what he had done" (vv. 12–13). Many other passages of Scripture teach that the final judgment deals with sins actually committed during our earthly existence.[3]

R. A. Webb correctly draws the proper inference from these texts when he declares "that future and final retribution will be [proportional] to 'deeds done in the body.'" But, he continues, "dead infants have been prevented by the providence of God from committing any responsible deeds of any sort in the body, and consequently infants are not damnable upon *these premises*; and there is no account in Scripture of any other judgment based upon any other grounds."[4] The basis of the final judgment will be actual sins committed during our earthly existence, something no deceased infant or mental incapable could do.

According to David Russell, a nineteenth-century Scottish author,

> God deals with His creatures according to what they are, and have done: and therefore He does not charge them with an actual transgression til once they have committed it. . . . In regard, therefore, to actual transgressions, the scriptures call them innocents, and, describe them as not knowing "either good or evil," and of course incapable of personal sin.[5]

It is true, Russell adds, that had such infants survived and lived to adulthood,

> they would have become actual transgressors; but God will not punish them on account of what they would, in that case, have done, for he judges his creatures according to what they are, and have done,—not according to what, without the aid of his special grace, they would do.[6]

A number of Christian thinkers have attempted to assign deceased infants and mental incapables to a much larger group that includes adults outside the normal bounds of Christendom who die without hearing the gospel.[7] This rather sloppy thinking is then offered as a possible reason why millions of pagan adults might be found in heaven even though they never heard or responded to the gospel. But it ought to be obvious that we are not dealing with members of the same group.

John Cumming, an American who wrote on this subject a century and a half ago, noted that when such passages as Romans 1 talk about pagans,

> the language is clearly dealing with responsible adults who have within their bosoms, consciences to accuse or excuse the guilty. But these characteristics do not belong to infants. They cannot be the subjects in any sense of such a responsibility. They are unconscious of the distinctions that subsist between right and wrong. They do not comprehend the authority, nature, and obligations of law, unless vaguely and dimly. They cannot, therefore, be classed with unevangelized heathens at the judgment-day. . . . They can be accused neither of rejecting the gospel nor of violating the law.[8]

Adults who die in an unbelieving, unregenerate state have rejected the truth God revealed in general revelation (see Romans 1) and have committed evil deeds in the body and hence are judged justly, according to the passages of Scripture quoted above. Deceased infants and mental incapables did not. Pagan adults in full possession of their mental faculties must not be thought of as the moral equivalent of infants. To describe any persons as morally incompetent, they must be mentally deficient in some way. This deficiency might result from some condition that has prevented them from reaching mental maturity. Pagans who can think like an adult are responsible and moral persons who can be judged justly for their deeds.

One more important point under this heading deserves mention. According to R. A. Webb, if a deceased infant

> were sent to hell on no other account than that of original sin, there would be a good reason to the divine mind for the judgment, but the child's mind would be a perfect blank as to the reason of its suffering. Under such circumstances, it would know suffering, but it would have no understanding of the reason for its suffering. It could not tell its neighbor—it could not tell itself—why it was so awfully smitten; and consequently the whole meaning and significance of its sufferings, being to it a conscious enigma, the very essence of penalty would be absent, and justice would be disappointed of its vindication.[9]

Consequently, Webb concludes, an unregenerate infant "cannot die in infancy: such a result would defeat the ends of justice. Consequently ... all infants dying in infancy are elect[10], redeemed, regenerated and glorified. . . . The death of an infant, therefore, is the [irrefutable] *proof* of its salvation."[11]

3. REGENERATE INFANTS

Several biblical passages tell of unborn infants whom God has blessed with a special relationship to himself. The prophet Jeremiah provides one such instance when he reports how "the word of the LORD" came to him, saying, "Before I formed you in the womb I knew you, before you were born I set you apart; I appointed you as a prophet to the nations" (Jeremiah 1:5). An even more important example of this kind of prenatal sanctification occurs in the case of John the Baptist. Of him it was said, "He shall be filled with the Holy Ghost, even from his mother's womb" (Luke 1:15 KJV).

These verses offer two examples of infants who were chosen by God for salvation before they were even born. The verses report that these infants were regenerated and sanctified by God's grace before birth. Had either child died in infancy, there can be no question as to his eternal destiny. If this sort of thing happens even once, it can certainly happen in other cases.

Some readers may not have noticed these verses before and may be unsure what to make of them. I promise to tie all of this together in the next two chapters.

4. JESUS AND LITTLE CHILDREN

Three well-known passages from three of the Gospels provide the last important point in my argument. I quote them in order:

> Then little children were brought to Jesus for him to place his hands on them and pray for them. But the disciples rebuked those who brought them. Jesus said, "Let the little children come to me, and do not hinder them, for the kingdom of heaven belongs to such as these." When he placed his hands on them, he went on from there (Matthew 19:13–15).

> People were bringing little children to Jesus to have him touch them, but the disciples rebuked them. When Jesus saw this, he was indignant. He said to them, "Let the little children come to me, and do not hinder them, for the kingdom of God belongs to such as these. I tell you the truth, anyone who will not receive the kingdom of God like a little child will never enter it." And he took the children in his arms, put his hands on them and blessed them (Mark 10:13–16).

People were also bringing babies to Jesus to have him touch them. When the disciples saw this, they rebuked them. But Jesus called the children to him and said, "Let the little children come to me, and do not hinder them, for the kingdom of God belongs to such as these. I tell you the truth, anyone who will not receive the kingdom of God like a little child will never enter it" (Luke 18:15–17).

There has been some disagreement over the meaning of the phrase "the kingdom of heaven belongs to such as these." Some have suggested that Jesus' point was that only people who are like little children will be in heaven. In other words, according to this interpretation, Jesus had no intention of teaching that all deceased infants will be in heaven, only that adults must become as trusting as children in order to be saved. While it is hard to argue with the relevance of such a message to arrogant, self-centered, skeptical adults, there is more going on in these verses. The interpretation that applies Jesus' words only to adults fails to deal adequately with two other occurrences mentioned in the passages: Jesus' indignation toward his disciples, and his special blessing for the children.

If the only purpose served by the children in these instances was their serving as examples or models of what true believing adults must become, then we must assume that Jesus was indignant at his disciples only because they stood between Jesus and examples of the kind of people who will be in heaven. That doesn't make much sense. What makes better sense is that the children in question had a special relationship to Jesus. Jesus was indignant because his disciples were sending away children, some of whom were "children of God"—that is, recipients of God's saving grace. It is hard to read these verses without seeing that they talk not only of mature adults who must become childlike but also of children who were already members of Jesus' kingdom.

John Calvin, the sixteenth-century reformer whose views about infant salvation are often misunderstood, wrote some interesting comments on these verses:

> This narrative is highly useful; for it shows that Christ receives not only those who, moved by holy desire and faith, freely approach unto him, but those who are not yet of an age to know how much they need his grace. Those *little children* have not yet any understanding to desire his blessing; but when they are presented to him, he gently and kindly receives them, and dedicates them to the Father by a solemn act of blessing. We must observe the intention of those who present the children; for if there had not been a deep-rooted conviction in their minds, that the power of the Spirit was at his disposal, that he might pour it out on the people of God, it would have been unreasonable to present their children. There is no room, therefore, to doubt, that they ask for them a participation of his grace.[12]

Calvin infers from Jesus' laying hands on and blessing the children that God's grace "is extended even to those who are of that age."[13]

In comments on Matthew 19:14, Calvin wrote that Jesus

> bears witness that He wishes to receive children, and in the end He both embraces them in His arms and blesses them by laying His hands upon them. From this we gather that His grace reaches to this age of life also. . . . It would be too cruel to exclude that age from the grace of redemption. . . . They [children] are renewed by God's Spirit according to the measure of their age until by degrees and its own time this power hidden within them increases and shines forth openly. . . . It is an irreligious audacity to drive from Christ's fold those whom He nursed in His bosom,

and to shut the door on them as strangers when He did
not wish to forbid them.[14]

It is also instructive to see the comments on our verses made
by Charles Hodge, the nineteenth-century Presbyterian we met
in the preceding chapter:

> The conduct and language of our Lord in reference to
> children are not to be regarded as matters of sentiment, or
> simply expressive of kindly feeling. He evidently looked
> upon them as the lambs of the flock for which, as the good
> Shepherd, He laid down his life, and of whom He said
> they shall never perish, and no man could pluck them out
> of his hands. Of such He tells us is the kingdom of
> heaven, as though heaven was, in great measure, composed
> of the souls of redeemed infants.[15]

An interesting connection exists between the gospel passages dealing with Jesus and infants and the last judgment passage found in Revelation 20. The books (note the plural) to be
opened before the Book of Life (note the singular) contain the
record of human deeds. The Book of Life contains the names
of all the born-again children of God. If Jesus meant to teach
that children are part of his heavenly kingdom, then the names
of these children are written in the Book of Life. But no one
whose recorded works constituted a rejection of God's truth can
appear in the Book of Life. Deceased infants can have no deed
recorded in the book of works, since they died before performing either evil or good works. Their lives were too short to allow
them to become moral agents. Thus, nothing written in the
book of works can apply to infants. Nonetheless, Jesus' observation that "of such is the kingdom of heaven" implied that at
least the names of the infants in his presence that day are written in the Lamb's Book of Life. Infants are saved because they
do not meet conditions for divine judgment. The reason this is

true is because infants lack the ability to behave in a morally responsible way.

EARLIER SUPPORTERS OF THIS BOOK'S POSITION

There is value, I think, in looking back and noting earlier advocates of the position defended in this book. Some of their comments add important information to what has already been presented in this chapter.

Some who deny the salvation of all deceased infants seek to exclude the children of unbelieving parents, about whom, they say, we must remain uncertain. The information we have reviewed in this chapter appears to contradict their claim. Charles Hodge wrote with great confidence that "All who die in infancy are saved."[16] He went on to note, "The Scriptures nowhere exclude any class of infants, baptized or unbaptized, born in Christian or in heathen lands, of believing or unbelieving parents, from the benefits of the redemption of Christ."[17]

John Newton, an eighteenth-century Anglican and the author of the words to such hymns as "Amazing Grace" and "Glorious Things of Thee Are Spoken," wrote,

> I cannot be sorry for the death of infants. How many storms do they escape! Nor can I doubt, in my private judgment, that they are included in the election of grace. Perhaps those who die in infancy are the exceeding great multitude of all people, nations, and languages mentioned (Rev. 7:9) in distinction from the visible body of professing believers who were marked on their foreheads and openly known to be the Lord's.[18]

Augustus Toplady, another Anglican composer of the eighteen-century and the writer of the words to the hymn "Rock of

Ages," declared his belief "that the souls of all departed infants whatever, whether baptized or unbaptized, are with God in glory. . . . I believe that in the decree of predestination to life,[19] God hath included all whom he hath decreed to take away in infancy."[20]

The position I affirm was also held by Benjamin B. Warfield, the great Princeton Seminary theologian whose teaching career included the last decades of the nineteenth-century and the early years of the twentieth.

CONCLUSION

My argument for the claim that all who die in infancy or in a congenital state of mental incapacity are saved has, in a sense, only begun. Even though the next two chapters will explore other important issues, those discussions will strengthen the case for infant salvation that I have begun in this chapter.

chapter six

INFANT SALVATION: SOME THEOLOGICAL ISSUES

Many Christians avoid theology the way they avoid trips to the doctor. They can always find excuses to put it off to another day. If such an attitude toward medical care is unwise, equally so is a dread of things theological. Hearken back to the earlier chapters of this book that illustrated, among other things, how various forms of theological illiteracy left grieving people at the mercy of those who would place them and their loved ones in spiritual jeopardy. Perhaps the theological topics we will discuss in this chapter and the next are not quite as critical as the issues discussed in the first half of the book. But it is still true that when it comes to theology, what you don't know *can* hurt you.

Chapters 1 through 4 helped us understand why several widely held attempts to ground infant salvation are failures. In chapter 5 I presented my answer to the question of infant salvation and offered arguments in support of it. In this chapter and the next we will examine how the two theological systems that dominate evangelical theology, Calvinism and Arminianism, deal with the issue of infant salvation.

It is one thing to assert the claim that "All children who die in infancy are saved." It is quite another to frame one's answer within the bounds of a sound theological system that supports that claim. Our investigation into the question of infant salvation cannot reach closure until we see which of these two theological systems is more faithful to Scripture and provides the more adequate ground for the salvation of infants and the mentally incapable.

A TALE OF TWO SYSTEMS

Protestant theology has been divided for centuries by a dispute between Calvinism and Arminianism. Calvinism (sometimes called Reformed theology) takes its name, of course, from John Calvin, the great sixteenth-century French reformer who lived the last decades of his life in Geneva, Switzerland. Arminianism takes its name from Jacob Arminius, a Dutch thinker who died in 1609.[1] As part of its distinguishing characteristics, Arminianism emphasizes human free will while Reformed theology places its emphasis on the glory and sovereignty of God. Although Arminians will object to the following statement, I can testify, as a former Arminian, that it is true: *When it comes to a forced choice*[2] between exalting God and exalting man, Arminians choose the latter. The argument for this claim will appear throughout this chapter and the next.

These two chapters are necessary because only one of our two systems can be true. What if we discover that Arminianism, the theological system of millions of evangelical Christians, cannot provide a ground for infant salvation? Would this information be important? What if we discover that only Reformed theology (Calvinism) can offer an adequate ground for the doctrine of infant salvation? Would it not be important to learn more about this second system?

THE DOCTRINE OF TOTAL DEPRAVITY

The term *original sin* refers to the fact that every human being since Adam (but excluding Jesus Christ) is born with a sinful nature. Even infants enter this world with an inborn tendency to sin (see chapter 1). The term *total depravity* refers to the fact that every human being is corrupted by sin in every facet of his or her being. Contrary to a popular misconception, Reformed Christians do not believe the doctrine of total depravity means that every human is as evil as he or she could possibly be.

Imagine two glasses of pure water into which someone then drops different amounts of black ink. The water in one glass ends up being significantly darker than the other. Yet, however different the water in our two glasses may appear, every molecule of water in each glass has been tinted by ink. If the ink is analogous to human sin, we could say that each glass of water is totally depraved, because the ink has contaminated every molecule of water in each glass. Similarly, even though human beings manifest differing degrees of sinfulness, it is still true that sin affects, taints, corrupts, and influences every facet of our being. Theologian Roger Nicole explains that the doctrine of total depravity means

> that evil is at the very heart and root of man. It is at the very foundation, at the deepest level of human life. This evil does not corrupt merely one or two or certain particular avenues of the life of man but is pervasive in that it spreads into all aspects of his life. It darkens his mind, corrupts his feelings, warps his will, moves his affections in wrong directions, blinds his conscience, burdens his subconscious, afflicts his body. There is hardly any dimension of man in which the damaging character of evil does not

manifest itself in some way. Evil is like a root cancer that extends in all directions within the organism to leave its devastating effects.[3]

Given this universal human problem, it is understandable why Scripture describes us as dead (Ephesians 2:1, 5; Romans 5:12), bound (2 Timothy 2:25–26), blind and deaf (Mark 4:11–12), unteachable (1 Corinthians 2:14), and sinful, both by nature (Psalm 51:5) and by action (Genesis 6:5).[4] This account of humanity's inherently sinful condition leads W. J. Seaton to ask, "Can the DEAD raise themselves? Can the BOUND free themselves? Can the BLIND give themselves sight, or the DEAF hearing? Can the SLAVES redeem themselves? Can the UNINSTRUCTABLE teach themselves? Can the NATURALLY SINFUL change themselves?"[5] It was this human hopelessness that Jeremiah had in view when he wrote, "Can the Ethiopian change his skin or the leopard its spots? Neither can you do good who are accustomed to doing evil" (Jeremiah 13:23). Job 14:4 makes the same point: "Who can bring what is pure from the impure? No one!"

The doctrine of total depravity demonstrates the utter inability of humans to please God through their own efforts. No human would or could seek God's forgiveness and salvation unless first moved by God. Perhaps nowhere in Scripture is human hopelessness and inability made more clear than in Ephesians 2:1–2: "As for you, you were dead in your transgressions and sins, in which you used to live when you followed the ways of this world and of the ruler of the kingdom of the air, the spirit who is now at work in those who are disobedient."

Picture someone who has rather significant gifts as a preacher and evangelist. Suppose that this speaker strides into a funeral home, steps in front of a casket, and begins preaching to the corpse. He uses his funniest stories, but the corpse does not laugh. He repeats his saddest illustrations, but the corpse does not weep. He gives his most powerful invitation, but the corpse does not respond. The apostle Paul teaches in Ephesians 2 that every unregenerate person is a corpse in the spiritual sense. As Seaton explains,

> We are like Lazarus in his tomb; we are bound hand and foot; corruption has taken hold upon us. Just as there was no glimmer of life in the dead body of Lazarus, so there is no "inner receptive spark" in our hearts. But the Lord performs the miracle—both with the physically dead, and the spiritually dead.[6]

This account of total depravity is one of the fundamental tenets of Reformed theology. According to Calvinism, humans are incapable of doing anything to bring about their salvation. When we are regenerated, it is because God convicts us of sin, enables us to understand the gospel, and produces the repentance and faith that leads us to Christ.

THE WESLEYAN VIEW OF TOTAL DEPRAVITY

One of the major reasons why so many people fail to heed the basic message of Reformed theology is that they do not understand or accept the fundamental fact of total depravity. Fallen human beings do not find it easy to admit they are in such a hopeless state. Contrary to Scripture, they still want to believe that human beings can bring themselves to do something that will lead to their salvation. The Christian church is full of preachers and laypeople who present the gospel to persons who are every bit as dead spiritually as a corpse is dead physically; they suppose that their wit, compassion, and eloquence ought to bring that spiritually dead corpse to a "decision for Christ."

I am not saying that such Christians are wrong in present-
ing the gospel to lost men and women. God commands us to do
this. It is the context of their service that is faulty. The actions of
such people show that they really do not believe in total depravity. When we finally understand the doctrine, we will come to
see that salvation is and must be the exclusive work of God—
from start to finish. Only God can raise the dead, and only God
can give life to the spiritually dead (Ephesians 2:6–7).

Things get a bit sticky at this point, so it is important to
pay attention. Because Arminianism is such a broad movement,
there is value in narrowing the focus to the Wesleyan version of
the system.[7] Wesleyan Christians who follow more or less the
thinking of John Wesley typically believe in both original sin
and total depravity. Their emphasis on human free will, however, requires them to make a move that effectively removes
total depravity from the table. If all humans are as spiritually
dead as the Bible teaches, human beings lack totally any ability
to play a role in their own salvation. While Wesleyans believe
in original sin,[8] they cannot accept a depravity so total that it
deprives the human will of the power to choose or reject God.
They believe that when a human being is regenerated, it is
because God did some things (such as sending his Son) and
humans do the rest (such as repenting and believing). Such acts
as repentance and faith are our contribution to our salvation.

Wesleyans negate *total* depravity through a teaching called
"prevenient grace." Thomas R. Schreiner provides a helpful
summary of this doctrine:

> What is common in all Wesleyan theories of prevenient
> grace is that the freedom, which was lost in Adam's sin, is
> sufficiently restored to enable people to choose salvation.
> Prevenient grace provides people with the ability to choose
> or reject God. As sinners born in Adam, they had no abil-

ity to do good or to choose what is right. But as recipients of prevenient grace they can once again choose the good.[9]

Wesleyans believe that by means of prevenient grace God counteracts the negative effects of human depravity in such a way as to allow mature human beings to stand in a position of relative neutrality with respect to God's salvation. Whether such people choose to believe or not is up to them.

Reformed Christians, by contrast, believe that salvation is due exclusively to God's grace, that it is a consequence of actions set in place by God, and that God's call to those he has chosen overcomes any opposition and resistance that the sinful person chosen by God might raise. Arminians believe that humans have the power to resist God's call to salvation. They interpret the biblical passages that mention predestination and election as references to divine actions based on God's knowledge of what humans will do in the future.[10] In other words, a person's coming to faith is not something made necessary by God's choosing that person. Instead, God's election is a consequence of what God knows that person will freely choose to do.

GOD'S WORK IN SALVATION

Reformed Christians believe, then, that salvation is totally and exclusively the work of God. As Seaton puts it, "If man is, indeed, dead and held captive, and blind etc., then the remedy for all these conditions must lie outside man himself [that is, with God]."[11] It should be obvious therefore, that God must initiate salvation. Salvation must be the work of God and God alone.

So what has God done to save us? The Reformed answer is that he chose us to be the recipients of his grace. Out of the entire company of human beings, God chose some to receive his gift of eternal life. Obviously, this implies that he also chose to pass by the rest of our species; only some members of the human race are included in his plan of salvation. Then, at a time of his own choosing, God sent his Son to earth to die for the sins of those whom God chose to be his children. Finally, God gave his Spirit to apply the results of Christ's atonement to everyone chosen by him. All of this is taught in several familiar passages of Scripture:

> And we know that in all things God works for the good of those who love him, who have been called according to his purpose. For those God foreknew he also predestined to be conformed to the likeness of his Son, that he might be the firstborn among many brothers. And those he predestined, he also called; those he called, he also justified; those he justified, he also glorified (Romans 8:28–30).

> For he [God] chose us in him before the creation of the world to be holy and blameless in his sight. In love he predestined us to be adopted as his sons through Jesus Christ, in accordance with his pleasure and will—to the praise of his glorious grace, which he has freely given us in the One he loves (Ephesians 1:4–6).

> But you are a chosen people, a royal priesthood, a holy nation, a people belonging to God, that you may declare the praises of him who called you out of darkness into his wonderful light. Once you were not a people, but now you are the people of God; once you had not received mercy, but now you have received mercy (1 Peter 2:9–10).

> Therefore, my brothers, be all the more eager to make your calling and election sure. For if you do these things, you will never fall, and you will receive a rich welcome into the eternal kingdom of our Lord and Savior Jesus Christ (2 Peter 1:10–11).

Because of their fundamental commitment to the role of human autonomy and free will in salvation, Arminians have to find a way to get around such passages. Their typical move is to reduce God's "election" to a response he makes to his knowledge of future human decisions. For the Arminian, the order is (1) a human being chooses to repent and believe in Jesus; (2) God foresaw this human decision; and (3) on the basis of his foreknowledge, God then elects the individual who he already knows will be saved in the future. Frankly, I consider this is a strange use of the words *elect, choose,* and *predestinate.* It is also important to notice that in order for (1) to occur, the individual human who possesses the power (free will) to believe or not to believe must be in a state quite removed from the total depravity described in Ephesians 2:1–2. This, as we have seen, is one consequence of what is typically called "prevenient grace."

According to Roger Nicole, Reformed Christians believe that

> the sovereign initiative in salvation is with God. It is not with man. God does not save a man by virtue of something that God has foreseen in him, some pre-existing condition which is the source or root of God's elective purpose. In his own sovereign wisdom God chooses those who shall be saved, for reasons that are sufficient unto himself.[12]

God's choice of those who will be saved has absolutely no basis in the merit of the person.[13]

Those who claim that God elects those whose faith he foresees miss one of the clearest and most important teachings of Scripture. God's choice is not based on anything a person does in the past, present, or future, including whatever acts of faith and repentance might lie in that time frame. Salvation is based totally upon God's grace: "For it is by grace you have been saved, through faith—and this not from yourselves, it is the gift of God—not by works, so that no one can boast" (Ephesians 2:8–9). Even the faith that saves us comes from God and is a gift of God.

IS SALVATION A JOINT EFFORT BETWEEN GOD AND HUMANS?

Reformed Christians believe that no human, adult or child, can be saved apart from God's choosing them, Christ's dying for them, and the Holy Spirit's calling them. Arminians disagree. The Arminian defense of human autonomy is part of their attempt to make humans into partners with God in their salvation, by means of human free will. Arminians teach that Christ died for all humans, not simply the elect; they believe that humans have the power to resist God's call; and that God's "election" is based completely on his foreknowledge of what humans will do in the future. They also diminish human depravity so that no human weakness might stand in the way of humans exercising their free will and becoming partners with God in their salvation.

Arminians believe that Christ's atonement produced only the possibility of salvation. This possible salvation can be turned into actual salvation only when humans use their free will to repent and believe. Arminians believe that God limited himself when he allowed free will; God cannot unconditionally save anyone without that person's consent. But now the very serious problem of infant salvation enters the scene. The Arminian view that has just been explained has to be altered to meet the needs of infants who die before they are able to do what adults can supposedly do. Arminians admit that the saved state of every infant is not a consequence of the child's free consent.

ARMINIANISM'S PROBLEM WITH
INFANT SALVATION

I have just explained what happens when the Arminian makes human repentance, faith, and perseverance in obedience a condition of God's foreknowledge and election. Arminians teach that only humans who perform such actions can receive the benefits of Christ's death. But it then follows that infants cannot receive these benefits, since they are incapable of repentance, belief, and obedience. Infants cannot be saved in a way that satisfies Arminian theology, because they lack the mental, moral, and physical ability to meet the conditions of Arminian salvation.

It is not difficult to see the problem that the Arminian emphasis on human free will creates regarding infant salvation. Since Arminians reject God's unconditional election as a necessary condition for salvation and since infants are incapable of understanding the gospel and responding to it in an act of free will, how can any infant be saved? How can an Arminian account for the salvation of all the mentally impaired and all the children who die in infancy?

Benjamin B. Warfield expressed this problem,

> If only a single infant dying in irresponsible infancy be saved, the whole Arminian principle is traversed. If all infants dying such are saved, not only the majority of the saved, but doubtless the majority of the human race hitherto, have entered into [spiritual] life by a non-Arminian pathway.[14]

Arminians cannot consistently believe that any human being, child or adult, can be a passive recipient of salvation; human beings must always be active initiators in the act of regeneration. For Arminians, active repentance and belief are necessary conditions of salvation. But how can this be possible for infants and mental incapables? How can an infant be saved if it cannot believe? How are infants and the mentally impaired delivered from their sinful nature, given their inability to produce acts of repentance and faith? If Arminians allow for the possibility that God might save even one human without its consent, without it being an active participant in its salvation, the Arminians are abandoning the essential core of their theology. After all, nothing, in the Arminian scheme of things must supersede the free will of the saved person.

If Arminians attempt to circumvent this problem by denying the depravity of infants and mental incapables, they have adopted the Pelagian heresy that we have already discussed. If Arminians postpone the possibility of infant salvation to some period of time after death, they commit the same errors as the post-death salvationists. That is, they admit that their theological system does not have an answer for the issue of infant salvation in this life; and they also adopt a theory that lacks biblical support and conflicts with the plain sense of Scripture, as we observed in chapter 3.

This seems to leave Arminians with only one other option, namely, to believe that the depravity of deceased infants and mental incapables is dealt with exclusively as an act of God's grace. But this is the Calvinist answer, not an Arminian one.

THE REFORMED VIEW OF
INFANT SALVATION

If we take the Arminian view of things off the table and examine the question of infant salvation from the Reformed perspective, we have quite a different situation. If Christ died specifically for those whom God chose or elected, then infant salvation becomes possible, because God in his grace is fully capable of electing infants as well as adults. As long as we think salvation depends on *our* doing something that only a rational adult can do, it should be obvious that infants who cannot perform those actions are beyond the reach of God's salvation. If humans must do some act that only a mature, rational person can perform in order to become the beneficiary of God's redemption, it is clear that no infant can be saved. But if we assume that salvation results from *God's* activity and that humans are the recipients of God's gracious acts, we can see how infants, not only adults, can be recipients of that grace. It is certainly clear that infants and mental incapables cannot cooperate with God in human salvation, as is required in the Arminian scheme of things.

INFANTS ARE CAPABLE OF SALVATION

Infants are capable of salvation. We observed this in the preceding chapter in the cases of John the Baptist and Jeremiah. In this chapter we have seen the biblical reason for this. Infants can be saved because they can be the object of God's gracious election, an election that has no basis in any human merit or accomplishment. An infant may be the beneficiary of election by God the Father, of atonement by God the Son, and of regeneration by God the Spirit. All three divine acts are unconditional and not dependent on human action.

R. A. Webb argues,

The infant, therefore, though incapable of "works" of any kind, may be a subject of grace—may be operated upon by the influence of the Holy Spirit, and changed and fitted, as an infant, for a life in heaven. Its heart may be regenerated; to it the atoning righteousness of Christ may be divinely imputed, as the ground of its justification; a child may be adopted into the family of God, even as it is adopted into a human family.[15]

But, many will wonder, what about faith and repentance? After all, infants are incapable of both. Webb explains, "Faith and repentance are not the meritorious grounds of salvation, but . . . only instruments—merely connectives—in the bringing into *consciousness* the benefits of the atonement of Christ. Their office is not to save, but to reveal salvation in human experience."[16] Since infants die before they are capable of faith and repentance, these instruments have no function in their case.

CONCLUSION

Benjamin Warfield provides a helpful summary of the ground we have covered to this point: "If all that die in infancy are saved, it can only be through the almighty operation of the Holy Spirit, who works when, and where, and how He pleases, through whose ineffable grace the Father gathers these little ones to the home He has prepared for them." The doctrine of infant salvation, Warfield concludes, "can find such a place in the Reformed theology. It can find such a place in no other system of theological thought."[17]

Reformed theology does not avoid the issue of infant salvation, but faces it directly and fully in a way that satisfies the demands of Scripture and historic Christian belief. There is nothing in the logic of the Reformed faith that entails the loss of one dead infant or mental incapable. Instead, I have argued, Calvinism is the theological system that best provides adequate biblical and theological grounds for such a doctrine. If people seek a basis for infant salvation outside the Reformed faith, they have only three options: Either they lapse into one of the forms of heresy criticized in chapters 1 through 4, or they conclude that all children who die in infancy are lost (because they can-not meet the conditions of Arminian salvation), or they acknowledge that they have no way of making their theory of infant salvation understandable. When it comes to finding a ground for infant salvation within the bounds of the historic Christian faith, the choice is either Calvinism or agnosticism.

chapter seven

THE REFORMED VIEW OF INFANT SALVATION

Now that we have seen that Arminianism lacks a consistent answer to the question of infant salvation, we face the separate challenge that makes this chapter necessary. If someone rejects the Reformed view of salvation, he or she must also reject the Reformed answer to the issue of infant salvation. But I have already demonstrated the failure of the theories that many people turn to today. What we are left with is this: If the Reformed view of infant salvation also fails, then we have no answer to the question of what happens when infants and the mentally incapable die.

The purpose of this chapter, as short and incomplete as it must be, is to show that people who are serious enough about the matter to look can find answers to all or most of their questions about the viability of the Reformed view of salvation and, subsequently, the Reformed view of infant salvation.

A BRIEF TESTIMONY

I spent many years of my adult life as an Arminian. Some readers may find helpful an account of the reasons and circumstances that led me finally to abandon Arminianism in favor of the Reformed position. There were four major reasons.

Reason No. 1. I stopped fighting the plain sense of Scripture. You must remember that I have been a professor of philosophy for more than forty years. Typically in my career, I have observed the requirement of keeping an open mind on a subject and thinking through problems before reaching a position. But my opposition to Calvinism was an exception. Only once before 1970, as I recall, did I open a book defending the Reformed position. As I skimmed through the book, I was unable to break the Arminian paradigm to which I was captive. The same problem existed whenever I came upon some "Calvinist" verse or passage in the Bible; I simply found a clever way to remove the Reformed sting from the text. I had convinced myself that Calvinism couldn't be true, and nothing—not even the abundance of biblical testimonies to God's grace—could change my mind.

The day finally came when I stopped running away from chapters like John 6, Romans 8, and Ephesians 1–2. I wasn't there yet, but my mind was no longer closed on the subject.

Reason No. 2: One day, while reflecting on the whole matter, I became conscious of the real nature of my struggle. I was torn between one position that exalted man and another that exalted God. Somewhere along the line I decided that since I had to choose between two such systems, I would finally get on God's side. That decision still makes sense to me.

Reason No. 3: Once I started seriously to read books by Calvinists, the writings of two Reformed thinkers began to break down my resistance. One of them was Roger Nicole in his essay titled "The 'Five Points' and God's Sovereignty."[1] The other was the well-known English theologian and author, J. I. Packer. Ironically, the Packer composition that helped me on the matter at hand was a short essay that few people have read.

It was published as a contemporary introduction to the reissue of a very old book by the seventeenth-century Puritan writer John Owen. The book is titled *The Death of Death in the Death of Christ.* Once I finished Packer's introductory essay, I kept reading Owen's work, and by the time I was finished I found myself in an entirely new world, one in which I was no longer an Arminian.

Reason No. 4: With my rejection of Arminianism now far behind me, I have found strong confirmation for my decision in the actions of many current Arminian thinkers. Keep in mind that one reason for my decision was my recognition that Arminianism exalted man at God's expense. In the past decade this march toward the exaltation of human autonomy and the diminishment of God has grown so reckless, I believe, as to justify doubts about the orthodoxy of some of these leaders.

One feature of the new Arminianism is a position called "inclusivism," which teaches that it is no longer necessary to believe that unevangelized pagans need to hear and believe the gospel in order to be saved. Another aberration is a denial that God has perfect knowledge of the future. When God's perfect knowledge of future human actions is thought to be a restraint on human free will, the new Arminians have a simple answer: Simply deny that God possesses such knowledge. These new versions of Arminianism sometimes travel under the banner of "the Openness of God." I will not say more about this except to add that in my judgment, some of the new Arminians are promoting a finite God who is so limited that I often feel led to pray *for* him and not *to* him.[2]

A SUMMARY OF PACKER'S ARGUMENT

Given the importance of Packer's work in my abandonment of Arminianism, I am sure the reader can understand why I find it important to summarize his argument here. It should be easy to see how that argument matched my mood and thinking as represented above in Reason Number 2.

J. I. Packer argues that Arminianism alters the content of Christian theology so dramatically as to create what he calls a new gospel. According to Packer, the central reference of the *old* gospel (that is, what he believes was the teaching of the apostles and the Reformers) was God. The purpose of this old gospel was "always to give glory to God. It was always and essentially a proclamation of Divine sovereignty in mercy and judgment, a summons to bow down and worship the mighty Lord on whom man depends for all good, both in nature and in grace."[3]

But the center of reference for the new gospel of Arminianism is not God, but man. The purpose of this new gospel is to help people feel better, not teach them to worship God. The subject of the new gospel is not God's sovereign ways with man, but the help God offers to men.

Packer points out that the advocates of Arminianism's new gospel

> appeal to men as if they had all the ability to receive Christ at any time; [they] speak of His redeeming work as if He had done no more by dying than make it possible for us to save ourselves by believing; [they] speak of God's love as if it were no more than a general willingness to receive any who will turn and trust; and [they] depict the Father and the Son, not as sovereignly active in drawing sinners to themselves, but as waiting in quiet impotence "at the door of our hearts" for us to let them in.[4]

The old gospel—that is, the Reformed gospel—grounds salvation on the work of God while the new gospel makes salvation dependent on a work of man. The old gospel views faith as an integral part of God's gift of salvation while the new gospel sees faith as man's role in salvation. The old gospel gives all the praise to God while the newer one divides the glory between man and God. The new gospel refuses to take sin and human depravity very seriously.

The new gospel, Packer continues,

> compels us to misunderstand the significance of the gracious invitations of Christ in the gospel. . . . [We] now have to read them, not as expressions of the tender patience of a mighty sovereign, but as the pathetic pleadings of an impotent desire; and so the enthroned Lord is suddenly metamorphosed into a weak, futile figure tapping forlornly at the door of the human heart, which He is powerless to open.[5]

Packer judges such thinking to be "a shameful dishonour to the Christ of the New Testament."[6] Moreover, the new gospel

> in effect denies our dependence on God when it comes to vital decisions, takes us out of His hand, tells us that we are, after all, what sin taught us to think we were—masters of our fate, captains of our souls—and so undermines the very foundation of man's religious relationship with His Maker.[7]

Roger Nicole is troubled by how close the new gospel comes to resembling the ancient heresy of Pelagianism by speaking

> as if man had a right to come into the presence of God and enter into account with him, as if God had some obligation to deal with all people in the same way. The one thing God owes us is judgment. We ought to marvel at the fact that instead of confining us all to judgment and

damnation, God in his mercy has been pleased to make plans to save a great multitude.[8]

Today I wonder how it could have taken me so long to see such a simple but important truth. But at least I see it now. And the position holds the answer for the question of infant salvation.

AN OBJECTION TO CALVINISM:
DID CHRIST DIE FOR EVERYONE?

If someone took a poll among opponents of Reformed theology as to their major objection to the system, the winner would be what is sometimes called the doctrine of "Limited Atonement." Arminians clearly dislike any suggestion that Jesus really did not die for everyone—but consider that every biblical Christian believes that Christ's atonement is limited in some sense.

Evangelical Arminians reject universalism, the belief that eventually every human being will be saved (see chapter 2). When Arminians admit that there are people who will not be saved, they are teaching their own version of a *limited* atonement. In their case, it is the efficacy of Christ's atonement they limit. Not every human will be saved. Christ died for all humans, they insist, but it is the individual person's fault that he or she does not take advantage of that atonement. Everyone is potentially saved, but that potential salvation becomes actual only in the case of people who repent and believe. As we saw in the preceding chapter, this seems to leave deceased infants and mental incapables in the lurch.

Reformed Christians are troubled by the Arminian picture of a God who wants to save humans but just cannot manage to pull it off in many cases. Arminians give us a picture of a God who wants to save Joe, Bill, and Mary. But if this trio wants to resist God, they can, and God will be helpless to do anything to overcome their resistance. So Joe, Bill, and Mary end up beyond the limits of Christ's atonement.

Calvinists believe that the Bible gives us a different picture. In this scenario, every human being chosen by God will be saved. Everyone for whom Christ died will be saved. Jesus, Calvinists believe, is a Savior who really saves; he does not simply stand there with his arms open, pleading with sinners to exercise their free will and come to him.

My point is that the phrase *limited atonement* has outlived its usefulness. After all, both Calvinists and Arminians limit the atonement in some way. The expression only muddies the waters. Of course, it does allow Arminians to present themselves as proponents of an "unlimited atonement;" but this amounts largely to just a verbal game.

It is for this reason that Roger Nicole suggests we use a different term to describe the Reformed position: *definite* atonement. In this view, Christ's atonement is definite in the sense that he died for a specific group of people, namely, those given him by God the Father. Jesus said in John 6:37, "All that the Father gives me will come to me, and whoever comes to me I will never drive away." If Calvinists are proponents of a definite atonement, this appears to leave Arminians as defenders of an *indefinite* atonement. If Calvinists believe that Christ died for a specific group of people, this leaves Arminians teaching that Christ died for no one in particular.

The Reformed position holds, then, that Christ died to save a particular group of people—the very people, it turns out, who were chosen by God before the universe was created. As Ephesians 1:4 states, "For he chose us in him before the creation of the world to be holy and blameless in his sight."[9] In John 17, Jesus prayed,

> "I have revealed you to those whom you gave me out of
> the world. They were yours; you gave them to me and they

have obeyed your word. Now they know that everything you have given me comes from you. . . . I pray for them. I am not praying for the world, but for those you have given me, for they are yours" (vv. 6–7, 9).

Everyone for whom Christ died will be saved.

Are there any biblical texts that teach a universal or indefinite atonement? The answer of Reformed Christians, not surprisingly, is no. Three verses are often appealed to by Arminians, as follows:

> ". . . God our Savior, who desires everyone to be saved and to come to the knowledge of the truth" (1 Timothy 2:3–4 NRSV).

> "He is the atoning sacrifice for our sins, and not for ours only but also for the sins of the whole world" (1 John 2:2 NRSV).

> "For the grace of God has appeared, bringing salvation to all" (Titus 2:11 NRSV).

The feature common to these and other texts that supposedly support the universal accessibility of salvation is the use of words such as *all* and *world*, which Arminians insist must always mean every human person. But it is not at all clear that this is what these texts mean. Consider Titus 2:11. How can the expression *all* really refer to every single human being who has ever lived or will live? That would require Arminians to teach either (a) that every human being who ever lived is saved; or (b) that the good news of salvation has actually reached every human being who has lived. But (a) is simply another formulation of the universalism we rejected in chapter 1; the claim is false. Indeed, it is heresy. Let us rush to say that Arminians do not wish to assert (a). But (b) is also false because, as everyone knows, millions of people never heard the gospel. What Titus

2:11 says is that the grace of God has brought salvation to all kinds of people; it does not mean that the grace of God has brought salvation to every single individual who has ever lived.

Calvinists point out that expressions like *all* may refer either to *all humans without distinction* or *to all persons without exception.* In their view, texts such as Titus 2:11 do not describe what God has done or is doing for all humans without exception— that is, for every single human being. Rather, the texts report what God did for all human beings without distinction. That is, Christ did not die just for Jews or for males or for educated people or for powerful individuals. He also died for Gentiles, for women and children, for barbarians, for slaves and the poor. He died for Jews, yes; but he also died for Romans, Thracians, Syrians, Ethiopians, Macedonians, and Samaritans. All these passages—Titus 2:11; 1 Timothy 2:3–4; and 1 John 2:2—tell us what God has done for all human beings without distinction.[10] Careful study will show, I believe, that Calvinists get the better of this argument.

ARE HUMANS MERELY PUPPETS IN GOD'S HAND?

Let us see where we are. Reformed thinkers argue that our fallen human nature makes it impossible for humans to save themselves. Indeed, we are in such bad shape morally and spiritually that we cannot even take one step in any supposed cooperation with God. If even one human is to be saved, God must initiate the process—and he did. God took that first step in purposing to save a specific group of individuals, including both adults and children who would die in infancy. Since salvation is the work of God and God alone, then God must produce a way by which he brings people to receive the salvation he provided on the Cross.

The nature of that process introduces us to another reason why many people resist the logic of the Reformed position. They insist on representing the Reformed view of this process as a kind of mechanical manipulation that turns people into puppets. But the idea of mechanical manipulation of people is a stereotype, a misrepresentation of what every Reformed thinker has taught. As Roger Nicole states, "The grace of God does not function against our wills but is rather a grace which overcomes the resistance of our wills. God the Holy Spirit is able to accomplish this."[11]

I believe that Nicole is quite correct when he says,

> I am not concerned about God's modes of operation, and I am quite ready to grant that he may well have a good number that I do not know about and that I am not able to explore. I do know that when there is resistance, God comes in with his mighty grace and subdues that resistance. He makes no one come against his will, but he makes him will to come. He does not do violence to the will of the creature, but he gently subdues and overcomes human resistance so that men will gladly respond to him and come in repentance and faith. We ought not to give the impression that somehow God forces himself upon his creatures so that the gospel is crammed down their throats, as it were. In the case of adults (those who have reached the age of accountability) it is always in keeping with the willingness of the individual that the response to grace comes forth.[12]

Nicole insists that any attempt to portray humans as mere puppets on a string does major violence both to the Reformed position and to the Scriptures that teach God's effectual grace.

ANOTHER OBJECTION: CALVINISM
IMPLIES THAT PEOPLE ARE SAVED
WITHOUT THEIR CONSENT

Another complaint against Calvinism is that the Reformed account of human redemption excludes any consent from those who are saved. The response that R. A. Webb made to this complaint almost a century ago is still relevant today. He began his reply by noting that

> God made Adam—without his consent. . . . He defined all the conditions of the trial in Eden—without his consent. He appointed his Son to be the sinner's Redeemer—without any man's consent. He sent his Spirit into the world—without the world's consent. He convicts and converts sinners—without their consent. . . . He has never appeared as a God limited and conditioned by the consent of his creatures. How much less does he have to get the consent of the helpless baby, before he can save the little thing from eternal death?[13]

Webb then added,

> Not even an adult can consent to the gospel arrangement, except the Spirit persuade and enable him: and if he [God] can, and does, quicken the soul of the adult sinner, often hardened and fixed in its iniquitous ways, it would seem to be even an easier task to quicken the spirit of the baby. If Christ bears the adult in his arms, I see not why it would not be a lighter load to carry the infant.[14]

Since this is how God deals with adults whom he has chosen, called, and brought to spiritual life, why should it be so difficult to see him dealing with infants and the mentally handicapped in the same way? "The glory of our gospel," Webb concludes, "is that it saves those who cannot save themselves: adults cannot save themselves, and infants cannot save themselves: if saved at all, both classes must be subjects of God's operations upon their natures."[15] The Arminian complaint about any absence of human consent in God's plan of redemption works no better than anything else we have encountered.

THE ATTEMPT TO EQUATE INFANTS AND UNEVANGELIZED ADULTS

Even though I have already dealt in chapter 4 with the matter of equating infants and unevangelized adults, the issue shows up with such frequency in contemporary Arminian literature that it merits one last look. A number of today's Arminian thinkers want us to believe in a theory called *inclusivism,* which is to say that millions of unevangelized adults in the Third World will be in heaven even though they never heard the gospel or exercised explicit faith in Jesus Christ. These Christian inclusivists seek to gain support for their position by equating deceased infants and unevangelized pagan adults. In other words, they say, if there will be dead infants in heaven who never heard the gospel, repented, and trusted Christ, we have a precedent for believing that unevangelized pagan adults will also be saved.

Almost a century ago, R. A. Webb saw through this manuever. Infants and the mentally disabled, Webb said, "are morally incompetent because they have not an intelligent and efficient grasp upon their mental faculties."[16] Webb makes it clear, however, that "*heathen* adults, who are in the normal and balanced possession of their faculties, are not moral infants."[17] Nor can pagan adults be grouped with mentally handicapped adults. "To pronounce any class of persons moral incompetents there must be an antecedent mental deficiency—a deficiency due to incomplete growth, or arrested development, or constitutional derangement. That heathen adult, who speaks as a man, understands as a man, and thinks as a man, is a responsible moral" person.[18] It is time for Arminians to acknowledge the weakness of this argument.

DOES THE WESTMINISTER CONFESSION TEACH THAT SOME DECEASED INFANTS ARE NOT ELECT AND THUS ARE NOT SAVED?

Even though the Westminster Confession (1648) is acknowledged as the primary theological statement of biblically faithful Presbyterians, it is respected by Reformed Christians of other denominations. Is it true that such an important statement of Reformed belief teaches that some dead infants are not elect and thus unsaved?

The key sections of the Confession that are the focus of this dispute read as follows:

> All those whom God hath predestined unto life, and those only, He is pleased, in His appointed and accepted time, effectually to call, by His word and Spirit. . . . so they come most freely, being made willing by His grace. . . . Elect infants dying in infancy are regenerated and saved by Christ, through the Spirit who worketh when, and where, and how He pleaseth (Westminster Confession of Faith, X, 1 and 3).

A number of people have attempted to use the words in X, 3 as proof that the Confession implies that some children who die in infancy are not elect and thus lack any hope for salvation. I consider this very bad logic. The sentence in question says, "Elect infants dying in infancy are regenerated and saved by Christ. . . ." These words clearly teach that some children who die in infancy are in heaven. But nothing in this statement rules out the possibility that *all* such infants[19] are elect and thus will be in heaven. Therefore the argument comes to naught.

CONCLUSION

Deceased infants and the mentally impaired are saved because God elected them, Christ redeemed them, and the Holy Spirit regenerated them. Using words from R. A. Webb, I offer one final attempt to make apparent the logic of God's plan of redemption.

> The Calvinist holds that the purpose of God is as wide at one end as it is at the other. . . . that God determined to save every one who is saved; that the population of heaven and the people of the decree are numerically and personally identical. . . . They rejoice to think that none of God's loved ones are lost; that there are no failures in his redemptive plan; that he undertook the salvation of no person, and then failed to make good his effort: that he is a being who never breaks down, because of blunder, nor because of weak incompetence; that he fulfills every promise, and brings to glory every person, upon whom he has set his affection; that he is not a being of afterthoughts, perpetually adjusting his plans, and shifting his procedures, to fit emergencies and altered circumstances; but that with him all is inerrant forethought; knowing the end from the beginning. The Calvinistic logic is inexorable—*what was last in execution was first in intention.*[20]

It should now be obvious that the question of infant salvation is not an isolated Christian doctrine. It is inseparably linked to God's plan of redemption for adults as well as children.

chapter eight

SOME FINAL QUESTIONS

In this final chapter I want to address several issues that are related to what we have been thinking about in this book. The first deals with the question of whether we will know each other in heaven. Naturally, the relevant point here is whether parents will know their children. The second concerns whether human relationships such as marriage and parenthood will continue in heaven. The third deals with the stage of maturity we will possess in heaven and how this might affect children who died in infancy. That is, will people appear at the same age that they were when they died, or have we reason to think some other age might apply? The fourth concerns the years during which children lack the mental and moral abilities necessary for being a moral agent.

WILL WE KNOW EACH OTHER IN HEAVEN?

It seems pretty clear that before we can know if the redeemed in heaven will know one another, we first have to know whether humans will retain their identity after death. Whether it be at the Last Judgment or in heaven, will we be the same people that we are in this life?

A good theological reason[1] to believe we will be the same people has to do with the justice of God's judgment at the end of history. Every human being will be raised from the dead and will stand before God at the judgment. It should be obvious that the person God judges at that time must be identical with the person who performed the deeds that he is judging. Similarly, the people whose names are written in the Book of Life must be identical with the individuals whom God elected and then called to faith and salvation.

An important biblical support for our belief in personal identity can be found in Jesus' words in Mark 12:26–27: "Now about the dead rising—have you not read in the book of Moses, in the account of the bush, how God said to him, 'I am the God of Abraham, the God of Isaac, and the God of Jacob'? He is not the God of the dead, but of the living." Even though Abraham had been dead for centuries when God spoke to Moses, Jesus interpreted God's words to Moses to mean that Abraham still existed *as Abraham*. Abraham retained his identity after death. Moreover, Abraham kept the relationship with God that he had enjoyed during his earthly existence. Jesus therefore assured believers that death does not end human existence or personal identity.

Additional biblical support for our belief in the continuation of personal identity after death centers on the Bible's information about Jesus following his resurrection. The disciples knew and recognized the risen Christ (John 20:19–23, 26–29; Acts 1:3–10). Many Christian thinkers suggest that the glorified bodies of believers will have characteristics similar to those of Jesus' resurrected body.

WILL DEATH DO US PART?

In the same chapter of Mark's gospel, Jesus is quoted as saying something that has puzzled and concerned many believers.

Seeking to trick Jesus, the Sadducees had told him the story of a widow who married her husband's brother. Her second husband also died, following which she married the third brother, and so on until she had been the wife of seven brothers. And then the time came when the woman herself died. The Sadducees then confronted Jesus with their question: "At the resurrection whose wife will she be, since the seven were married to her?" (Mark 12:23)[2]

It is Jesus' answer that gives rise to our little problem: "Are you not in error because you do not know the Scriptures or the power of God? When the dead rise, they will neither marry nor be given in marriage; they will be like the angels in heaven" (vv. 24–25). It is easy to understand how loving spouses, parents, and grandparents might believe that Jesus was discussing the termination of their most important earthly relationships. In our case, do Jesus' words suggest an end to a parent's relationship to a beloved child who died in infancy?

But is that really what Jesus' words mean? Some rather simple distinctions will make clear, I believe, that Mark 12:25 has been misunderstood.

Some human relationships are primarily legal in nature. While the marriage relationship between a believing husband and wife ought to transcend the legal requirements of the state, it is impossible to ignore the legal dimension. This legal dimension is recognized in all kinds of ways, including tax responsibilities, inheritance, and property rights. The marriage must be recognized by the state; laws describe the rights and duties of each partner.

Some relationships are physical. The parent-child relationship, though carrying legal ties, is certainly physical. But is it merely physical? I suggest that in addition to its physical and legal aspects, the parent-child relationship can and should be a spiritual relationship. In this spiritual sense, being a mother or father entails more than the act of procreation. Some parents in the physical sense have never been parents in the spiritual sense; likewise, some children in the physical sense, through disrespect and lack of love, have disqualified themselves as children in the spiritual sense. Although adoptive parents can never become the physical parents of their adopted child, they can establish a spiritual parent-child relationship when they love that child as their own.

Given these distinctions, we are now in a position to understand Jesus' point in Mark 12:24–25. Obviously, death brings an end to legal and *merely* physical relationships. A natural way of understanding Jesus' words is that this suspension of physical and legal relationships continues after the resurrection. But there is no reason to suppose that spiritual relationships begun on earth are dissolved. Human beings who have had loving relationships on earth can believe with confidence that those spiritual relationships will continue. Even more, they can be confident that, without the sin that taints all of our earthly relationships, the fellowship to come will be more marvelous than anything we can comprehend at this time. Nothing Jesus said in Mark 12 provides the slightest justification for doubting that heaven will mean the reunion of husbands with wives, parents with children, grandparents with grandchildren, and friends with friends.

Also, let us not overlook what Jesus says in Mark 12:27, that God "is not the God of the dead, but of the living." The person who stands before the Lord at the final judgment will be the same person who committed the sins for which he or she is being judged. The person we encounter in heaven will be the same person we knew and loved on earth. And Jesus taught this in the very words that followed Mark 12:24–25. Jesus therefore assured believers that death does not end human existence or human identity, and that *spiritual* relationships begun on earth will continue in heaven.

WILL INFANTS STILL BE INFANTS
IN HEAVEN?

I confess that I do not find any specific illumination from Scripture on the question of whether infants will remain infants in heaven. I am reduced to offering some speculation, though I am confident that what I say will prove to be correct. And I will offer one supportive passage of Scripture.

First, the speculation: God's creation provides countless examples of how living things begin as a single cell and then develop to maturity. If an acorn is placed in an environment that allows it to develop to maturity, it will become an oak tree. But after a period of time, the oak tree will become diseased, will die, and will eventually decay. When was the oak tree at its best? In general terms, the answer seems clear even if some of the details might be difficult to explain.

The Bible describes the redeemed in heaven as possessing glorified bodies. Whatever the full meaning of this glorification means, it surely must include the fact that our glorified bodies will represent that dimension of our humanity *at its best.* I believe this means that children who die in infancy will greet us in heaven as mature adults, just as physically crippled adults and aged seniors who died feeble and frail will greet us "at their best." I believe that mentally impaired children and adults as well as aged seniors who died suffering from Alzheimer's disease or other failings of their mental faculties will greet us "at their best."

Revelation 7 contains perhaps the most complete and glorious picture of the redeemed in heaven:

> After this I looked and there before me was a great multitude that no one could count, from every nation, tribe, people and language, standing before the throne and in front of the Lamb. They were wearing white robes and

were holding palm branches in their hands. And they cried out in a loud voice:

> "Salvation belongs to our God,
> who sits on the throne,
> and to the Lamb."

All the angels were standing around the throne and around the elders and the four living creatures. They fell down on their faces before the throne and worshiped God, saying:

> "Amen!
> Praise and glory
> and wisdom and thanks and honor
> and power and strength
> be to our God for ever and ever.
> Amen!"

Then one of the elders asked me, "These in white robes—who are they, and where did they come from?"

I answered, "Sir, you know."

And he said, "These are they who have come out of the great tribulation; they have washed their robes and made them white in the blood of the Lamb. Therefore,

> "they are before the throne of God
>   and serve him day and night in his temple;
> and he who sits on the throne will spread his tent over
>   them.
> Never again will they hunger;
>   never again will they thirst.
> The sun will not beat upon them,
>   nor any scorching heat.
> For the Lamb at the center of the throne will be their
>   shepherd;

he will lead them to springs of living water.
And God will wipe away ever tear from their eyes" (vv.
9–17).

It is a great tragedy in my view that many Christians are misled into thinking that these saints in white robes are not the elect of God who make up his church, the bride of Christ.[3] The "great tribulation" mentioned in verse 14 is not some supposed period of seven years that still lies in the future. It is a reference to the entire period of history in which God's people have suffered for their faith.[4]

If, then, this passage in Revelation is a picture of redeemed saints in heaven, we must note that it contains no reference to infants, the physically disabled, or the mentally handicapped. On the contrary, the text provides support for the belief that in the glory of heaven, such redeemed infants will mingle their voices with those of their redeemed loved ones in the praise of the Triune God who effected their salvation.

The fact, therefore, that all life, including human life, develops through stages is relevant. The infant is supposed to grow into childhood, the child is to grow into adolescence, and the teenager is to grow into adulthood. Somewhere during the cycle of a human life, there is a stage of physical and mental maturity in which we will be as fit as we will ever be. Of course, this assumes that during the development of the person, nothing goes wrong. And that stage, we have good reason to believe, will be the state of the redeemed in heaven.

WHAT IS THE RELEVANT AGE FOR CHILDREN?

Many parents understandably would like to know the age at which children lose the moral and spiritual immaturity we have had in view throughout this book. It is important to realize that we may be talking about a spread of several years. Children mature at different ages because of such variables as home environment, religious training, education, and the nature of the society to which they belong. According to one theory, it is possible that children may reach this age more quickly in Christian homes. According to another, children reach this age more quickly now due to the influence of television, relationships with other children, and other facets of an increasingly corrupt society.

With some children, it might be the age of four or five; with other children, it might be a little later. But it should be obvious that nothing in this book provides warrant for parents to ignore the spiritual well-being of their children. If anything, one of the more important messages of this book is the urgency for parents to surround their children with a moral and spiritual environment that will encourage them to trust in God from their earliest days.

THE IMPORTANCE OF THE FAMILY

And the previous question leads naturally to my next point, the importance of the family. I recently came across an important idea in a little-known religious journal. After thinking a while about the evangelistic mission of the church, Robert Rayburn, the author of the article, suggests that the major factor used by God in the salvation of a vast number of the redeemed in heaven may be the effect godly parents have on their own children. In Rayburn's words, "Christian nurture in a godly home, beginning in infancy, is the divine instrumentality of the salvation of the church's children and that this nurture was the primary method appointed for the propagating of the church."[5]

To some extent, Rayburn is following here the views of such earlier Reformed thinkers as Benjamin Warfield and Herman Bavinck. Warfield made his point in saying that the family

> is the New Testament basis of the Church of God.... [God] does, indeed, require individual faith for salvation; but He organizes His people in families first; and then into churches, recognizing in their very warp and woof the family constitution. His promises are all the more precious since they are to us and our children. And though this may not fit in with the growing individualism of the day, it is God's ordinance.[6]

Bavinck put it this way: "The family is not of man's making; it is a gift of God and full of life. Upbringing in the family bears a quite special character. No school or educational institution can replace or compensate for the family."

Bavinck continued,

> Everything educates in the family, the handshake of the father, the voice of the mother, the older brother, the younger sister, the baby in the cradle, the sick loved one, the grandparents and the grandchildren, the uncles and the aunts, the guests and friends, prosperity and adversity, the feast day and the day of mourning, Sundays and workdays, the prayer and the thanksgiving at the table and the reading of God's Word, the morning and evening prayer. Everything is engaged to educate one another, from day to day, from hour to hour, unintentionally, without previously devised plan, method or system. From everything proceeds an educative influence though it can neither be analyzed nor calculated. A thousand insignificant things, a thousand trifles, a thousand details, all have their effect. It is life itself that here educates, life in its greatness, the

rich, inexhaustible, universal life. The family is the school of life, because there is its spring and its hearth.[7]

Rayburn is quite confident "that far and away the largest part of the Christian church at any time or place—excepting that historical moment when the gospel first reaches a place and people—are those who were born and raised in Christian families, and that this is true whether one is considering Christendom as an outward phenomenon or only the company of the faithful followers of Christ."[8] Christian parents have a God-given obligation to ground their children in the Christian faith. We should surround mentally impaired persons with an environment that teaches them of God's goodness, love, and grace.

God has given Christian parents the duty to instruct their children in "the works and will of God" and prepare them "for a life of faith," Rayburn writes.[9] He refers his reader to such passages of Scripture as Genesis 18:19; Exodus 10:1–2; 12:24–27; 13:8, 14–16; 31:12–13; Deuteronomy 4:9; 6:4–9; Psalm 44:1; 78:1–8; Isaiah 38:19; 2 Timothy 3:14–15. He observes that Scripture teaches that a Christian home "is to be both a school of faith and a temple in which the acknowledgement of God and his worship confirm and adorn the instruction."[10] And, of course, we should never forget that pastors and a family's congregation also have obligations under God for the nurturing of little ones.

THE QUESTION OF PRENATAL DEATH

At least one more important question needs an answer. What happens in the case of pregnancies that are terminated either by miscarriage or abortion? Are fetuses that die under such circumstances in the same condition as children who die in infancy? My wife and I share this concern with my readers because we lost a child by miscarriage very early in a pregnancy.

Before beginning my research on this book, I had often wondered if we might someday meet that child. Because I seem to have a vested interest in this matter, let me make it very clear that I have not allowed my heart and my emotions to determine my answer.

This section of the chapter was not part of the original manuscript and was added very late at the suggestion of the editors at Zondervan. When they raised the issue, I saw immediately that it was a question that needed comment.

The need for brevity forces me to limit my comments to two points. The first concerns what we know about the nature of prenatal life from the moment of conception. The second is a look at several major biblical passages that contain crucial information about the status of prenatal life.

Some Important Facts About the Sequence of Conception

We know five things about what happens at conception: (1) the human female's ovum contains 23 chromosomes; (2) the male's sperm contains 23 chromosomes; (3) the specific ovum and sperm no longer exist after conception; (4) what does exist is a single cell (zygote) with 46 chromosomes; (5) the zygote is alive, a fact seen in such events as metabolism, growth, reactions to stimuli, and reproduction by means of twinning—that is, the cell divides repeatedly, with all of the subsequent cells containing the same 46 chromosomes.

Because the growing and reproducing zygote has human parents for its cause, it is human life. Because the zygote's 46 chromosomes come from the chromosomes in the mother's ovum and the father's sperm, something else must be noted. As Francis J. Beckwith explains,

> The conceptus is a new, although tiny, individual with its own genetic code (with forty-six chromosomes), a code

that is neither her mother's nor her father's. From this point until death no new genetic information is needed to make the unborn entity an individual human. Her genetic makeup is established at conception, determining to a great extent her own individual physical characteristics— eye color, bone structure, hair color, skin color, suscepti-bility to certain diseases. That is to say, at conception, the genotype—the inherited characteristics of an individual human being—is established and will remain in force for the entire life of this individual. The unborn individual, sharing the same nature with all human beings, is unlike any individual who has been conceived before and is unlike any individual who will ever be conceived again (unless she is an identical twin).[11]

Beckwith goes on to note, "The only thing necessary for the growth and development of this human organism, as with the rest of us, is oxygen, food, and water."[12]

We must not get hung up on the fact that what I and others describe at this point as human life is but a single cell. Dr. Mor-ris Krieger, author of *The Human Reproductive System*, explains, "All organisms, however large and complex they may be when full grown, begin life as but a single cell. This is true of the human being, for instance, who begins life as a fertilized ovum."[13]

Biblical References to the Unborn

The Bible describes the unborn in ways that clearly imply humanity and personhood. Consider Psalm 139:13–16:

> For you created my inmost being;
>   you knit me together in my mother's womb.
> I praise you because I am fearfully and wonderfully
>   made;
>   your works are wonderful,

I know that full well.
My frame was not hidden from you
    when I was made in the secret place.
When I was woven together in the depths of the earth,
    your eyes saw my unformed body.
All the days ordained for me
    were written in your book
    before one of them came to be.

Writing under divine inspiration, the psalmist David claims identity with the preborn individual in his mother's womb. Noting this, John Jefferson Davis points out that

> David naturally acknowledges his personal history and identity to have begun in the womb. His language suggests that his personal identity is not restricted to his conscious memory, but extends back beyond conscious recollections to the earliest time of God's creative control of his prenatal development. These verses strongly imply that personal identity is a continuum, beginning in the womb and extending naturally into postnatal life.[14]

Something very similar appears in Jeremiah 1:4–5:

The word of the LORD came to me, saying,

> "Before I formed you in the womb I knew you,
> before you were born I set you apart;
> I appointed you as a prophet to the nations."

Along these same lines, it is worthwhile to look up Isaiah 49:1, 5.

Without question, the most significant biblical passage in this regard appears in the first chapter of Luke's gospel. From the context we know that Mary is very early in her pregnancy. Here is what we learn in Luke 1:39–45:

At that time Mary got ready and hurried to a town in the hill country of Judea, where she entered Zechariah's home and greeted Elizabeth. When Elizabeth heard Mary's greeting, the baby [known to us today as John the Baptist] leaped in her womb, and Elizabeth was filled with the Holy Spirit. In a loud voice she exclaimed: "Blessed are you among women, and blessed is the child you will bear! But why am I so favored, that the mother of my Lord should come to me? As soon as the sound of your greeting reached my ears, the baby in my womb leaped for joy. Blessed is she who has believed that what the Lord has said to her will be accomplished!"

When referring to Elizabeth's unborn child, Luke, a physician by occupation, used the Greek word *brephos* which in other texts is used of postnatal babies (see Luke 18:15; 1 Peter 2:2; and Acts 7:19).

As John Jefferson Davis sees it, texts such as Luke 1:39–45 and Jeremiah 1:4–5 indicate

that God's special dealings with human beings can long precede their awareness of a personal relationship with God. God deals with human beings in an intensely personal way long before society is accustomed to treat them as persons in the "whole sense." As with divine election, so with calling and consecration to service: God's actions present a striking contrast to current notions of personhood.[15]

To my mind, the evidence on display in this section carries unavoidable implications as to the immorality of abortion on demand.

To quote Davis one more time, such texts show

that categories normally applied to postnatal man are applied also to the unborn. Again, while some allowance must be made for the possibly metaphorical nature of such biblical statements, it is hard to resist the impression that God takes a deep interest in the unborn child. Even without constituting a strict proof of the personhood of the unborn child—at least in the very earliest stages of pregnancy—these texts do challenge traditional views of personhood. Far from showing that the unborn are *less* than persons, these texts appear, in fact, to point in the opposite direction.[16]

What conclusions should we draw from the information noted above? I cannot speak for all of my readers, but as for me and my house, I cannot reach any other conclusion but that life in the womb that is ended before birth is human life—and is so from the moment of conception. And if the argument of this book about infant salvation is sound—as I obviously believe it is—then prenatal human life that is terminated either by miscarriage or abortion falls under the same general conditions of divine election as applies in the case of children who die in infancy.

There is more going on in all this than another testimony to divine grace. It is also a matter of divine justice that the millions and millions of innocent babies who have been butchered and killed by abortionists are in heaven. We leave the killers of those babies to the judgment of God. May they seek forgiveness before it is too late.[17]

CONCLUSION

The local city newspaper recently carried a front-page picture of a young businessman emerging from his smashed automobile after a major accident on an interstate highway. As I looked at the picture, it was difficult to see how the man survived, let alone lived to walk away. Like most of us, I am sure, that man gave no thought to the possibility that his everyday commute to work might have meant the end of his life. The accident took seconds, but the result could have lasted for eternity.

All of us suffer from the tendency to take life and this day and the next moment for granted. But we shouldn't. Every day, little children die from one cause or another. Each morning and evening we should thank God for their presence in our lives and ask him for the grace to fulfill our biblical responsibility to raise them in such a way they will know and love him.

Would it not be a shame if some reader of this book does not know the Lord and is not a believer? Loving parents know how tragic it is to lose a child. But consider the tragedy of the parent whose separation from a saved infant will last for all eternity, simply because the child is saved and the parent is not. For such readers, this may be the time to close this book and reflect upon one's own relationship with Jesus Christ.

HEAVEN SCENT

A cold March wind danced around the dead of night in Dallas as the doctor walked into the small hospital room of Diana Blessing.[1]

Even while she was still groggy from surgery, her husband, David, held her hand as they braced themselves for the latest news.

That afternoon of March 10, 1991, complications had forced Diana, only twenty-four-weeks pregnant, to undergo an emergency cesarean to deliver the couple's new daughter, Danae Lu Blessing. In her being only twelve inches long and weighing only one pound and nine ounces, they already knew she was perilously premature.

Still, the doctor's soft words dropped like bombs. "I don't think she's going to make it," he said, as kindly as he could. "There's only a 10-percent chance she will live through the night, and even then, if by some slim chance she does make it, her future could be a very cruel one."

Numb with disbelief, David and Diana listened as the doctor described the devastating problems Danae would likely face if she survived. She would never walk. She would never talk. She would probably be blind. She would certainly be prone to other catastrophic conditions from cerebral palsy to complete mental retardation. And on and on.

"No . . . no!" was all Diana could say.

She and David, with their five-year-old son, Dustin, had long dreamed of the day they would have a daughter and become a family of four. Now, within a matter of hours, that dream was slipping away.

Through the dark hours of morning as Danae held onto life by the thinnest thread, Diana slipped in and out of drugged sleep, growing more and more determined that their tiny daughter would live—and live to be a healthy, happy young girl. But David, fully awake and listening to additional dire details of their daughter's chances of ever leaving the hospital alive, much less healthy, knew he must confront his wife with the inevitable.

"David walked in and said that we needed to talk about making funeral arrangements," Diana remembers. "I felt so bad for him because he was doing everything, trying to include me in what was going on, but I just wouldn't listen. I couldn't listen.

"I said, 'No, that is not going to happen, no way! I don't care what the doctors say. Danae is not going to die! One day she will be just fine, and she will be coming home with us!'"

As if willed to live by Diana's determination, Danae clung to life hour after hour, with the help of every medical machine and marvel her miniature body could endure. But as those first days passed, a new agony set in for David and Diana.

Because Danae's underdeveloped nervous system was essentially "raw," the lightest kiss or caress only intensified her discomfort—so they couldn't even cradle their tiny baby girl against their chests to offer the strength of their love. All they could do, as Danae struggled alone beneath the ultraviolet light in the tangle of tubes and wires, was to pray that God would stay close to their precious little girl.

There was never a moment when Danae suddenly grew stronger. But as the weeks went by, she did slowly gain an ounce of weight here and an ounce of strength there.

At last, when Danae turned two months old, her parents were able to hold her in their arms for the very first time. And two months later—though doctors continued to gently but grimly warn that her chances of surviving, much less living any kind of normal life, were next to zero—Danae went home from the hospital, just as her mother had predicted.

Today, five years later, Danae is a petite but feisty young girl with glittering gray eyes and an unquenchable zest for life. She shows no signs whatsoever of any mental or physical impairments.

Simply, she is everything a little girl can be and more—but that happy result is far from the end of her story.

One blistering afternoon in the summer of 1996 near her home in Irving, Texas, Danae was sitting in her mother's lap in the bleachers of a local ballpark where her brother Dustin's baseball team was practicing. As always, Danae was chattering nonstop with her mother and several other adults sitting nearby—then suddenly fell silent.

Hugging her arms across her chest, Danae asked, "Do you smell that?"

Smelling the air and detecting the approach of a thunderstorm, Diana replied, "Yes, it smells like rain."

Danae closed her eyes and again asked, "Do you smell that?"

Once again, her mother replied, "Yes, I think we're about to get wet. It smells like rain."

Still caught in the moment, Danae shook her head, patted her thin shoulders with her small hands, and loudly announced, "No, it smells like *him*. It smells like God when you lay your head on his chest."

Tears blurred Diana's eyes as Danae happily hopped down to play with the other children before the rains came. The girl's words confirmed what Diana and all the members of the extended Blessing family had known, at least in their hearts, all along.

During those long days and nights of her first two months of her life when her nerves were too sensitive for them to touch her, God was holding Danae on his chest—and it is his loving scent that she remembers so well.

NOTES

PROLOGUE — When a Baby Dies

1. The testimony of the Cupschalks is used with their permission.

CHAPTER ONE — Are Children Born Without Sin?

1. The one exception here, of course, is Jesus Christ.

2. For a book-length defense of the claim that Scripture is the Word of God, see Ronald Nash, *The Word of God and the Mind of Man* (Phillipsburg, NJ: Presbyterian and Reformed, 1992). For a more compact version of this defense, see Ronald Nash, *The Closing of the American Heart* (Richardson, TX: Probe Books, 1990), chapter 11.

3. R. A. Webb, *The Theology of Infant Salvation* (Richmond, VA: Presbyterian Committee of Publications, 1907), 267.

CHAPTER TWO — Universalism: Will Everyone Be Saved?

1. Readers interested in more information about the theories attributed here to Reverend Matthews should consult Ronald Nash, *Is Jesus the Only Savior?* (Grand Rapids: Zondervan, 1994).

CHAPTER THREE — Salvation After Death?

1. We must never forget Scripture's dire warnings about humankind's sinful state. See Ephesians 2:1–9 as just one example.

2. "The spirits in prison" passage is supposed to be a reference to Christ's descent into hell following his death.

3. For a list of other verses that teach this same truth, see my discussion in chapter 4.

4. The verse says nothing about how much time might elapse between death and the final judgment.

5. For a more detailed discussion of the doctrine of salvation after death, see Ronald Nash, *Is Jesus the Only Savior?* (Grand Rapids: Zondervan, 1994).

CHAPTER FOUR — Does Baptism Save?

1. Luther's *Catechism*, Part IV, 2.

2. *The Augsburg Confession*, Part I, Art. 9.

3. See the records for the Fifth Session, Section 3; the Seventh Session, Can. 5; and the Twenty-first Session, Chapter 4.

4. Quoted by T. M. De Ferrari, "Baptism (Theology of)," in *New Catholic Encyclopedia*, vol. 2 (Washington, DC: Catholic University of America Press, 1967), 64.

5. H. Mueller, "Baptism (in the Bible)," in *New Catholic Encyclopedia*, vol. 2 (Washington, DC: Catholic University of America Press, 1967), 55.

6. See De Ferrari, "Baptism (Theology of)," 63.

7. R. A. Webb, *The Theology of Infant Salvation* (Richmond, VA: Presbyterian Committee of Publications, 1907), 235–36.

8. Ibid., 236.

9. Some of the very churches that insist on infant baptism have become uncomfortable with denying salvation to unbaptized infants in other religions. For example, many Protestants do not know that Roman Catholicism allows some exceptions to baptismal regeneration, apparently unconcerned with the apparent inconsistency this implies. For a helpful discussion of these exceptions (called "baptism by blood" and "baptism by desire"), see Harold O. J. Brown's chapter, "Unhelpful Antagonism and Unhealthy Courtesy," in the book *Roman Catholicism*, ed. John Armstrong (Chicago: Moody Press, 1994), 163–78.

10. Charles Hodge, *Systematic Theology*, vol. 3 (reprint, Grand Rapids: Eerdmans, 1975), 593.

11. Ibid.

12. Ibid., 598–99.

13. Most modern commentaries on Mark's Gospel provide details about this textual problem.

14. Hodge, *Systematic Theology*, 602.

15. Ibid.

16. Ibid., 602–3.

CHAPTER FIVE — A Case for Infant Salvation

1. Theologian R. A. Webb offered a helpful definition of the kind of mentally challenged persons I have in mind. The person in question "is an instance of arrested mental development ... [who thus] lingers in the region of intellectual childhood" (R. A. Webb, *The Theology of Infant Salvation* [Richmond, VA: Presbyterian Committee of Publications, 1907], 4).

2. My sentence uses "good acts" and "evil acts" in a way that presupposes that the agent or person performing the deed acts intentionally and with the knowledge that the deed is right or wrong.

3. See Jeremiah 17:10; Ezekiel 18; Matthew 16:27; Romans 2:6, 8; Galatians 6:7–8; and Revelation 22:12.

4. Webb, *The Theology of Infant Salvation*, 42.

5. David Russell, *Infant Salvation; Or, An Attempt to Prove That All Who Die in Infancy are Saved,* 3d ed. (Glasgow: James Maclehose, 1844), 47. Russell refers readers to Jeremiah 19:4 and Deuteronomy 1:39.

6. Ibid.

7. For more on this issue, see Ronald Nash, *Is Jesus the Only Savior?* (Grand Rapids: Zondervan, 1994), chapter 8.

8. John Cumming, *Infant Salvation; or All Saved that Die in Infancy* (Philadelphia: Lindsay and Blakiston, 1855), 36–37.

9. Webb, *The Theology of Infant Salvation*, 288–89.

10. I will explain the meaning of *election* in the next two chapters.

11. Webb, *The Theology of Infant Salvation*, 291.

12. John Calvin, *Calvin's Commentaries. A Harmony of the Gospels, Matthew, Mark and Luke,* vol. 2 (Grand Rapids: Eerdmans, 1972), 388.

13. Ibid., 388.

14. Ibid., 251–52.

15. Charles Hodge, *Systematic Theology,* vol. 1 (Grand Rapids: Eerdmans, 1975), 27.

16. Ibid., 26.

17. Ibid.

18. John Newton, *Works,* IV, 182.

19. I will explain Toplady's reference to predestination in the next two chapters.

20. *The Works of Augustus Toplady* (New ed., London, 1837), 645, 646.

CHAPTER SIX — Infant Salvation:
Some Theological Issues

1. Arminius was known by several other names, but there is no need to complicate things with that information.

2. A "forced choice" is one where there is no third alternative.

3. Roger R. Nicole, "The 'Five Points' and God's Sovereignty," in *Our Sovereign God*, ed. James M. Boice (Grand Rapids: Baker, 1977), 30. The chapter appears on pages 29–36.

4. I have borrowed this helpful analysis from W. J. Seaton, *The Five Points of Calvinism* (London: Banner of Truth, 1970), 6.

5. Seaton, *The Five Points of Calvinism*, 6.

6. Ibid., 7.

7. Wesleyanism also exists in several different forms, but we cannot talk about everything.

8. Which is another way of saying they want to distance themselves from Pelagianism.

9. Thomas R. Schreiner, "Does Scripture Teach Prevenient Grace in the Wesleyan Sense?" in *The Grace of God, the Bondage of the Will*, vol. 2, ed. Thomas R. Schreiner and Bruce A. Ware (Grand Rapids: Baker Books, 1995), 372. Three additional comments: (1) both volumes of this excellent work provide clear and insightful discussions of many important issues in the Calvinist-Arminian debate; (2) Schreiner's chapter (pp. 365–82) provides a fair picture of the doctrine of prevenient grace along with helpful bibliographic notes that will direct interested readers to many of the best books on the subject; (3) Schreiner, in my opinion, succeeds in showing that there is no biblical support for the doctrine of prevenient grace.

10. A number of influential Arminian thinkers have begun to teach that God does not have knowledge of future human actions. Clearly, such a position imposes severe limitations upon God. If such thinkers are consistent, they cannot continue to base predestination on God's knowledge of the future. See Ronald Nash, *Is Jesus the Only Savior?* (Grand Rapids: Zondervan, 1994).

11. Seaton, *The Five Points of Calvinism*, 7–8.

12. Nicole, "The 'Five Points' and God's Sovereignty," 31.

13. See Deuteronomy 7:7–8; Romans 9:15–16, 21; and Ephesians 1:4–5.

14. Benjamin B. Warfield, "The Development of the Doctrine of Infant Salvation," in *Two Studies in the History of Doctrine* (New York: Christian Literature Co., 1897), 230.

15. R. A. Webb, *The Theology of Infant Salvation* (Richmond, VA: Presbyterian Committee of Publications, 1907), 208.

16. Ibid., 281.

17. Warfield, "The Development of the Doctrine of Infant Salvation," 238–39. This long essay (covering pages 143–239 of this book) has been reprinted a number of times, sometimes in a slightly abridged form.

CHAPTER SEVEN — The Reformed View
of Infant Salvation

1. Roger Nicole, "The 'Five Points' and God's Sovereignty," in *Our Sovereign God*, ed. James M. Boice (Grand Rapids: Baker, 1977).

2. For more information about these trends, see Ronald Nash, *Is Jesus the Only Savior?* (Grand Rapids: Zondervan, 1994), and Millard Ericson, *The Evangelical Left* (Grand Rapids: Baker, 1997).

3. J. I. Packer, "Introductory Essay" to John Owen, *The Death of Death in the Death of Christ* (reprint, Edinburgh: Banner of Truth Trust, 1959), 2.

4. Ibid.

5. Ibid., 20.

6. Ibid.

7. Ibid.

8. Nicole, "The 'Five Points' and God's Sovereignty," 43.

9. See also Matthew 26:28 and Ephesians 5:25.

10. Readers interested in pursuing this matter further cannot do better than acquire a classic text on the subject by John Owen, *The Death of Death in the Death of Christ*. Owen provides a detailed analysis of "every" universalist text.

11. Nicole, "The 'Five Points' and God's Sovereignty," 33.

12. Ibid.

13. R. A. Webb, *The Theology of Infant Salvation* (Richmond, VA: Presbyterian Committee on Publications, 1907), 203.

14. Ibid., 204.

15. Ibid.

16. Ibid., 5.

17. Ibid.

18. Ibid.

19. Please note that the Confession is discussing infants who die in infancy. Neither the Confession nor I claim that *all* infants are elect. Obviously, millions of adults who are not saved were once infants.

20. Webb, *The Theology of Infant Salvation*, 271.

CHAPTER EIGHT — Some Final Questions

1. Students of philosophy know that human identity after death is also a philosophical problem. Since this is not a philosophy book, I will not discuss that issue here.

2. The Sadducees were theological liberals who did not believe in a bodily resurrection. In all likelihood, stories like this were given in an attempt to confound the faithful.

3. According to a different view of the end times, the people described in our text are martyrs killed during the so-called tribulation period.

4. For arguments that support this reading, see Ronald Nash, *Great Divides* (Colorado Springs: NavPress, 1992).

5. Robert S. Rayburn, "The Presbyterian Doctrines of Covenant Children, Covenant Nurture, and Covenant Succession," *Presbyterion* 22, no. 2 (1996), 86–87. Even though my use of this quote separates it from its context, there can be no doubt but that this is Rayburn's position.

6. Benjamin B. Warfield, "The Polemics of Infant Baptism," in *The Works of Benjamin B. Warfield*, vol. 9 (New York: Oxford University Press, 1932), 405–6.

7. Quoted in A. B. W. M. Kok, *Herman Bavinck* (Amsterdam: N.p., 1945), 1, 18, 19.

8. Rayburn, "The Presbyterian Doctrines of Covenant Children," 96.

9. Ibid., 103.

10. Ibid.

11. See Rayburn, "The Presbyterian Doctrines of Covenant Children."

12. Francis J. Beckwith, *Politically Correct Death* (Grand Rapids: Baker, 1993), 42.

13. Ibid.

14. Quoted in Beckwith, *Politically Correct Death*, 42.

15. John Jefferson Davis, *Abortion and the Christian* (Phillipsburg, NJ: Presbyterian and Reformed, 1984), 43.

16. Ibid., 49.

17. Ibid.

18. I want to express my appreciation to Dr. Francis Beckwith for his advice and assistance with this section.

EPILOGUE — Heaven Scent

1. This story comes unattributed from the Internet.

We want to hear from you. Plese send your comments about this
book to us in care of the address below. Thank you.

ZondervanPublishingHouse
Grand Rapids, Michigan
http://www.zondervan.com

A Division of HarperCollins*Publishers*